Phyllis Dawson Nicholls

# THE DIARY *of* PRIVATE AA BRIDGES

25th Field Service Garrison Battalion, Middlesex Regiment

Phyllis Dawson Nicholls

# THE DIARY of PRIVATE AA BRIDGES

25th Field Service Garrison Battalion, Middlesex Regiment

**MEREO**
Cirencester

## Mereo Books

1A The Wool Market Dyer Street Cirencester Gloucestershire GL7 2PR
An imprint of Memoirs Publishing www.mereobooks.com

The Diary of Private A A Bridges: 978-1-86151-256-7

First published in Great Britain in 2014
by Mereo Books, an imprint of Memoirs Publishing

The address for Memoirs Publishing Group Limited can be found at
www.memoirspublishing.com

The Memoirs Publishing Group Ltd Reg. No. 7834348

Cover Design - Ray Lipscombe

The Memoirs Publishing Group supports both The Forest Stewardship Council® (FSC®) and the PEFC® leading international forest-certification organisations. Our books carrying both the FSC label and the PEFC® and are printed on FSC®-certified paper. FSC® is the only forest-certification scheme supported by the leading environmental organisations including Greenpeace. Our paper procurement policy can be found at
www.memoirspublishing.com/environment

Typeset in 11/16pt Bembo
by Wiltshire Associates Publisher Services Ltd. Printed and bound in Great Britain by
Printondemand-Worldwide, Peterborough PE2 6XD

Dedicated to the men of the 25th Battalion,
Middlesex Regiment.

I would like to acknowledge my use of material
garnered from the Regimental Magazine and from
Colonel John Ward's book *Diehards in Siberia*.

From the Herts. *Advertiser and St Albans Times*
Rifleman Herbert (Bert) Bridges,
105 Verulam RoadAugust 1915

Mr and Mrs Herbert Bridges of 105 Verulam Road received a letter from the War Office this Friday morning which stated that their son Rifleman Herbert Grimwood Bridges (Bert) aged 24 of the 8th Batt Rifle Brigade has died of wounds. Rifleman Bridges was wounded on the 31st July near Ypres.

A message conveying the sympathy of the King and Lord Kitchener was also received. When Rifleman Bridges was wounded on July 31st near Ypres his parents had made an effort to have him brought home, but the wounds were too serious. In fact the deceased had been unable to write home at the time he was struck down. He had only been at the front four months and spent his 24th birthday in the trenches.

He joined the Army in London in December and tried to get to the Horse Guards but being unable to ride he transferred to the Rifle Brigade. Before enlisting he was employed by Mr D Mercer, Prospect Road, who has sent a touching letter of sympathy to the deceased parents. He was a member of the Conservative Club, from which quarter there have been many enquiries as to his condition during the time he lay wounded in hospital. The deceased hailed from Suffolk but the family has been in St. Albans for 17 years. Mr Bridges Sen. having been formerly employed under the late Sir J Blundell Maple at Childwickbury. The deceased was engaged to be married after the war to a young Newmarket girl who formerly lived at Childwickbury and who with her parents has paid a visit to Mr and Mrs Bridges in St. Albans this week. The deceased was a regular correspondent home. He used to write to his parents twice a week. When therefore, there was a sudden pause in the correspondence Mr and Mrs Bridges knew that something had happened to their son. And then came the news that he had been wounded.

Letters written by the deceased during July from "somewhere in Belgium" included the following extracts: "13th July 1915. No doubt you will have received my letter saying we came out of the Trenches On July 8th. It was shocking; worse than Hades. I can tell you, not one of us wants to go back to the same Trenches. They are Trenches captured off the Germans and awful ones too. The Town is a sight worth seeing, all battered to pieces, a big place too. Just as we were coming out of the trenches one chap, a brigade signaller, got hit by a shell that went right through him and did not explode. This was about ten yards in front of us, it was a sight. We were gassed everyday by Gas Shells, you will have seen that the Germans have used a lot of them lately. It does get into your eye sockets and makes them run, like a kid crying and makes them smart awfully. I shall be able to tell you about it when I get back, which I hope, will be soon. As you know I am in a telephone section now. We get better and more grub. The worst part of the job is mending the wires, which get broken very often by shells, especially at what they call "Hell Fire Corner" and "Suicide Corner".

July 22nd. Just a few lines to let you know that I am still knocking about somewhere in Flanders and also in the best of health. We are having some glorious weather too hot in the daytime though and too [cold?] at night. This is our last day in the rest camp. We go into the Trenches again tomorrow. I go in this time with a telephone section who are on duty night and day alike. Four hours on and four hours off. As it is my first go with them will tell you all when we come out again, which I have heard won't be for 21 days this time.

July 26th. I am quite all right and in the best of health. I have just been reading the St. Albans Times. Says they were 60 yds away from the [breaches] in places where we were, there are only 50 yds between us and you can stand on the Trenches and bomb one another. Just as I was completing your letter I saw a sight worth seeing, a German aeroplane brought down. I saw it burst into flames and spin in the air. You should have heard the cheers from the chaps said, "Straff 'em".

He is buried in Poperinghe New Military Cemetery, Belgium. The Abbey Parish Street Memorial in Verulam Road was dedicated in April 1921.

# Introduction

My book is based on the personal diary of a lonely soldier who, during the First World War, reached out to tell of his travels. It is laced with the newspaper cuttings he saved and articles taken from the Regimental Magazine in which other soldiers of various ranks wrote their views and experiences. Upon copying the diary and articles to combine them into the sequences of events without altering any of the words, the project became a journey back in time. The original writers portrayed humour and dignity without being vulgar in describing vulgarity, thus clearing the mind to listen to their cleaner descriptions. They turn us back from today, when perhaps too much is said, to earlier times when much is said in suggestion. The tale is told reliving the charm of the Victorian era, when a man was a gentleman and a woman was always a lady, when hardships were born with dignity and grace in public, while suffering and joy were private emotions for sharing with loved ones alone. Their outward calm and gentility served to spread courage and honour in troubled times and stressed a respectability this world may never know again.

The reality and horrors of war were lightly mentioned by the Tommies, while the tasks of each day were accomplished with good grace and optimism, in the belief that the war would soon be over. Life at the barracks became a continuing interest, while men who had thought they might never leave their home towns were sent on to new horizons, visiting strange lands, turning their army days into times worthy of recall.

This is a story of heroes without heroics, of men who thought themselves exempt from serving in the army with physical disabilities but were later reclassified as fit for restricted duties. Men who found themselves as far away from home as Siberia, where the fighting was as fierce as in any battle zone and the weather ran to incredible extremes, from tropical heat to freezing and raging blizzards, making conditions very much worse than those the troops had to bear while fighting in Western Europe.

These men first enlisted into a B1 classification, with the intention that they should replace the A1 men working on garrison duty. But their status changed whenever the need for a battalion of soldiers arose, and they viewed with wry amusement their ascents and descents on the scale of fitness. They had volunteered to serve their country under the Derby Scheme and answered the call again and again with courage and determination until after the end of the war.

Before we begin the journey of Private Bridges, we should be better off to learn a bit about the man who wrote the diary and consider the social structure of his day and the class into which he was born. In saying that he was a child of the Victorian era who had heard of the Boer War, survived the Great War, endured the Second World and the Korean War, we span his lifetime by outlining his years but tell us nothing of his days.

To describe his personality is to look into the make-up of his whole generation, for his nature was a pattern of his fellow man and his character was a stamp of his own. Private Bridges was many things. He was as smoothed and round as a football. His friends and relations never saw the inside of him, as his emotions were held in check always, his nature closed firmly around him.

He rolled through life, it seemed; sometimes he got tossed, now and then kicked, but he always bounced back for more, ready to score again.

He was a man of a peculiar breed of his time, a man who shyly turned from affection, repelled hugging and kissing and turned his back on close and personal involvement. He was restrained in both impulse and action, sitting back from adoration, seeking to be the onlooker rather than the one in the limelight. He shunned heroics, for whatever he did was all in the course of duty. He was a humble man.

Neither was he unfeeling or unkind, nor brash nor rude or demanding. He was tolerant, independent, stoic and stubborn, a proud man who had learned to guard what was his by keeping his possessions as proof for having his place in the world. What belonged to him was never made redundant or discarded; maybe put aside or laid away but never, never thrown away.

This remarkable man was born in times of a hardship we shall never see again. Within a decade or two there would be no one alive to recall those times. It was a time when everything gained was either paid for in cash saved from long hours of labour or fashioned by hand from raw materials with the simplest of tools, and only then if all the meagre priorities of living had been first met - not the desires of one man alone, but whatever the family needed, maybe money for the rent, the coal bill or sometimes bread for the table.

No matter what one's age or status, child or adult, single or married, everyone was responsible for the home and the family before all else. The working class was too poor to dare to get into debt. Whenever the money was all spent folks simply went without, and children knew the meaning of 'no'. Therefore every gain became a treasure: the loss of hard-earned chattels could mean further hardships and shame. Every tool was used with pride and care, accidents were avoided or unacceptable, and abuse was unforgivable.

Those were the days when man was measured by what he had, classed by his possessions. He strove to prove his worth, valued his self-esteem and respected the property of others. Nevertheless he was not without a sense of humour, or he could not have survived. He had a real capacity for wit, could laugh at his own misgivings, mock injustice and carry on with optimism and courage in the face of all odds.

Man enjoyed the simple things of life. The pleasures that cost nothing gave him rest from his labours and freed his mind from the burdens of poverty. He enjoyed the earth, the warmth of the sun and the babbling brook. The plants that grew from the soil gave him hope for things to come, while the rain, the wind and the snow were his reminders of the power of God. The singing of the birds was his music and the ringing of the church bells was solace for his soul.

In performing a task he did it conscientiously, for he believed that a job worth doing was worth doing well. There was little he asked of his neighbour for fear of imposing on his generosity, he expected no favours should he be unable to repay, and he was ever grateful for small mercies.

Should he be called upon to lend a helping hand, he would do so willingly, especially in labours of love to those in greater need than himself; for in times of unemployment, sickness and death hardships struck without mercy.

His needs and fears were no more and no less than his fellow man, so he learned early in life not to complain. In keeping his troubles to himself his strength was manifest in the pride that he carried his load without charity. What he feared most was hunger and humiliation. Though he was poverty stricken, he was at ease with life so long as he had the strength to fight his lot.

Such a man was born in the days of strictest class distinctions. Moulded into the working class, structured by the dictates of his needs, controlled by his abilities to provide, he did his best to pull himself up one step at a time. His rewards were firmer footholds in his world with the acceptance and loyalty of his class.

Into this class was born Private Bridges, and in this class he chose to remain all his life. A quiet, shy man, never gregarious, although he ran sometimes with the best, he was uncomfortable on the social ladder; his successes were in cherishing the prize of the moment. He was content to stay within the lines of his inheritance.

Old Uncle Alf was a little boy at the turn of the century. As a child he lived on the edge of a country village in Hertfordshire, on part of a large and picturesque estate, Childwickbury near Harpenden, which was owned by a very wealthy man. He grew into boyhood aware of the rich and in awe of their opulence. Though he never crossed the massive porticoes of the mansion, there is no doubt that he peered through the hedges of rhododendrons and stared wonderingly at the elegance before him.

His father was a groomsman for the master of the house, and the family lived in a tied cottage. He went to the village school and spent a childhood of carefree days walking along the country lanes and playing in meadows of buttercups and long grass. He climbed the trees in the copses, and played 'conkers' in the autumn. These were days before the motor car, when the roads were often dirt tracks for horse-drawn carts and the occasional carriage and pair.

As a small child he was fragile. Life for his mother and father was fraught with the struggles of the days when labour was cheap and unemployment ran high. His emergence into the world, along with his twin sister, must have added greatly to the burdens of the little family, who already had one son. Proper nourishment for a delicate child must have been prohibitive, for while his brother and twin grew straight, his legs were bowed with rickets.

Young Alfred grew stronger as he grew older. Playing in the sunshine, picking the blackberries from the hedgerows and mushrooms from the pastures, he must have skipped and jumped and run races with has friends with all the joy and enthusiasm of a child. By the time he was a young man he was competing in the local race meetings and bringing home prizes for his efforts. He was to become a dedicated marathon runner and an avid sportsman, enjoying the outdoors as often as he could.

Meanwhile the family had grown, with a little sister who became my husband's mother. Several years later another son was born to complete the family. By the time Alf finished school they had moved nearer the city, into a Victorian terraced house in St Albans. He worked as a butcher's boy for one of the local shops. He wore a blue striped apron over his grey serge suit, rode a bicycle with a large basket on the front and delivered fresh meat daily to the upper class houses in town.

During Alfred's working youth, besides his participation in marathon races he played with the Thursday Football League.

Such football teams were popular all over the country then, especially for the young shop assistants. Early closing day was on Thursday and the young people let loose during the week found the parks and the games an inexpensive way to channel their pent-up energy. Those who were not actually on the teams cheered for their side or strolled on the grounds with their sweethearts.

Times were hard indeed then. There was a time and place for everything and an orderliness, with rules and standards obeyed by most for fear of disgrace. My father recalls the young man who was invited to play in the Saturday League with a chance for a place with a national team on a professional basis. Alas for the lad, his father owned a grocery store, so he could not or would not spare him from behind the counter on the busiest day of the week. Fathers were strict and stern, their motives unquestioned, and sons were best to obey.

By the time the Great War began, Alfred was a young man. His older brother had been called to fight and had died on the field of battle. Poor eyesight had exempted Alfred from service, but after severe losses and the call under the Derby Scheme*

*The Derby Scheme was a scheme by which men volunteered their services as there was no conscription under the Liberal Government at that time. Men wore armbands which portrayed their willingness to fight, to counteract the stigma of being presented a white feather as an accusation of cowardice.

The Scheme was a method of obtaining recruits for the British Army during the First Great War. Towards the end of 1915 the numbers of recruits were below the point essential to the conduct of the war. The government decided to adhere to the voluntary system, and Lord Derby, as Director General of recruiting, devised the scheme

*known by his name. All men between 18 and 41 were invited to enlist,*
*and the recruits were then ranged in 46 age groups, 23 of married and*
*23 of unmarried men. They were to be called to the colours in groups*
*beginning with the younger men, the unmarried being called first. The*
*campaign began in October 1915. Men who came forward "attested"*
*and technically joined the army, but then returned home, wearing the*
*"Derby armlet" until called up. The total number who offered*
*themselves under the scheme was 2,829,263, of whom 1,679,263*
*were married. Moreover a number of the attested men were either*
*indispensable to civilian work or unfit. The result was a net addition to*
*the army of only about 850,000 men. According to the National*
*Register 2,182,178 remained unattested, of whom 1,152,947 were*
*single. Compulsion was therefore seen to be inevitable, and the*
*necessary bill was introduced into parliament on January 5 1916.*
*(Courtesy of Mirror Group Newspapers Limited)*

Alf, by his own admission, had been turned down by the army several times before they took him in. I don't know why. He was a bit short and a bit short sighted, and he stuttered too. Perhaps the army was so accustomed to interviewing fearsome fellows for the fighting forces that the little guys got overlooked. But when the cream of the crop was watered down, or more likely gunned down, the likes of Alf got a second chance, and the likes of Alf proved to be every bit as tough and capable in a fight as the big and burly boys.

In training camp he learned to fill his boots and fire a gun. In the face of danger, he was as brave as a giant. In England he was issued with kit and khaki and in Hong Kong he was issued with a new set of teeth and gold-rimmed glasses, all the better to see him through two years of turmoil. One thing I know for sure, he was a determined little man with strong legs and a heart of gold beneath his shy demeanour.

In signing up for the limited duties of a man in the B1 category, he enlisted with thousands of other willing young men to hold up the rear, taking over the work in the colony garrisons, while the regular soldiers took on the fight at the front.

The travels and experiences of Private A A Bridges and the British Tommies with whom he served cannot be better told than by the words they wrote themselves recording their wit and daring and deaths.

There follows a complete and accurate copy of the notes written by Alfred Arthur Bridges from the day of his induction into the army in 1916 until his release in 1919.

# ARMY CAREER

## OF PRIVATE A A BRIDGES
### 25TH BATTALION, MIDDLESEX REGIMENT, ALDERSHOT

Having been rejected several times before the Derby Scheme came into force, I was very doubtful as to my being accepted for service, but the Bedford Medical Board passed me for Garrison Duty abroad (B.1. Category) and on September 26th 1916 I was called to Watford, thence to Bedford, where I stayed for two days to get fitted out with Army clothes etc. Then I was ordered with a few more to proceed to Aldershot for training in the 25th Field Service Garrison Battalion, Middlesex Regiment.

Things were not as bad as I thought they would be, and I soon got used to the drills etc., and one sergeant of the Metropolitan Police Force, whose name was Gardiner was a rare barker, but a comic at the same time.

## PLYMOUTH

On the night of departure from Aldershot plenty of beer was knocking about and some took more than they could carry, but all is well that ends well, and we started for the station at twelve o'clock. Strange to say we lost our way as we took the wrong turning, but after a bit of roaming with kit bags and full packs we managed to find it alright, and one & all were absolutely tired out. The train ride was very nice and on arriving at Exeter ladies provided us with breakfast, after which we continued our journey, arriving at Devonport about 11.30 on the 24th December. We had Christmas Day on the *Tyndareus*, which was waiting for us on Plymouth Sound. After a few days there waiting for other ships, the convoy consisting of seven ships, all conveying troops started away on January 5th 1917 escorted by eleven destroyers.

Meanwhile in a South Coast town lived another man enlisting for the cause, who later was to write the following, which was published in the Regimental Magazine.

*From the Regimental Magazine*
MY FIRST IMPRESSIONS OF THE ARMY
BY L CORPL MC ALLISTER

As soon as Lord Derby's scheme for recruiting was made known to the public I attested. in fact I believe I was among the first half-dozen in the South Coast town in which I was living to offer to the land of my birth the assistance of which she stood - and for that matter still stands - in such dire needs. I might mention that I was in a very late group, and did not think that my services would be required for a very long time, if ever.

It came to me as a bit of a shock when some weeks later I received a form from the Ordinance Yard, Eastbourne, informing me that I had to report myself there at a certain date. This however, failed to cause me any great amount of trepidation, as I did not for one moment believe that I should ever be accepted, and dash it! I've got to break off now as First Post has just been sounded, my equipment is in pieces, I've lent my rifle to a man and have to borrow another before I can show myself on staff parade.

As I was saying when the First Post called me back to the path of duty, I never expected to be accepted; but I was and was classified B1. This is the first time I had heard of categories connected with the Army, but I "pinched" a card from a man which explained matters in a very concise manner. Those who had been passed A1 were sent to a different depot, while those in the B1 category heard with somewhat mixed feelings that Chichester was to be their resting place for a week, but that eventually they were to go on to Aldershot.

We got to Chi-Chi pretty late and were given a ticket each for a meal at the canteen, and we were able of course, to purchase any extras we required. Now at Chichester we got our first real impressions of the Army, and those with any perspicacity at all saw at once that "swank" wouldn't go down, and the wise ones dropped it at once.

There was an old gentleman as orderly in the hut to which I was told off. It had been my good – or bad – fortune during a somewhat varied experience to meet some ribald old blackguards: but for real blasphemy, I have no hesitation in awarding the palm to this old chap. He was a soldier of the old school, had been born and bred in the Army, knew his India well, and for rough kindness was hard to beat, though he tried his best not to show it, as he considered it weakness. But he had the one failing which I have mentioned, which combined with drink, made his conversation a dream of delight towards midnight.

I have met heavy drinkers, both before and since: but in this line "old Jack" was "on his own", and I would back him at "weight-for-age" against any man I have ever met.

I'll admit that I didn't think a great deal of "Jack" the next day either, as his expressions became even worse after the canteen had been open an hour, but I will say this for him - he had a very extensive vocabulary, and one never felt bored, though one frequently shuddered. I got to know the old chap better later on, however, when I caught him in a corner trying to comfort a youngster who had left home for the first time; and his voice, though the words were somewhat rough-hewn, was as gentle as a mother's, and I felt I knew "old Jack" better. When the time came to go to Aldershot I was genuinely sorry to leave him. Some of his yarns about the Afghan and Zulu wars were pretty mellow too. The British Army contains many such as he, and in the next world I expect to meet him, like Kipling's immortal Gunga Din,

"Squatting on the coals,

Giving drink to poor damned souls."

I should like to meet him again, however, before either of us leaves this one.

The day came when we all had to leave him, and Chichester was to know us no more. We learned in due course that Aldershot was our destination, and we left for there with more or less apprehension; but we were informed on the way down, by soldiers of the old army, that "The Shot" was pretty "cushy", and, looking back, I can say it wasn't half bad. I think it was a proud moment in the lives of a good many of us when we were served out with rifles and a full kit and when we began to "swank" around Aldershot with as much of it on as we were allowed to carry we voted the Army "not too bad", an opinion, however, which many have changed since then, or say they have.

The next day we were introduced to that prince of drill instructors, Sergeant Gardner. By the way, on our arrival at Aldershot we were met by the old R.S.M.Walsh, who somewhat paved the way for what we were to go through by telling us that "there was an instructor who wasn't really bad, though he was somewhat strict". We found this to be the case next day, when Sergeant Gardner took us in hand. Looking back, I don't think any of us have been through anything worse than we did that first week at Aldershot, and I wished myself dead then more than once. He started off by threatening to hit me over the head with that cane of his, and the way he showed his teeth and snarled made my blood run cold. I made a slight slip at the beginning of things by mistaking his order "Form Fours" for "Quick March", and when I started off on my own I really thought he was going to hit me.

Another joyful time we had was on the musketry course. In this "Standing Load" is varied with "Lying Load", which makes a welcome change, and this combined with picking up the "dummies" and re-inserting them in their clips makes the days pass very pleasantly.

Things improved gradually, however, and after we had been reduced to a state of abject subjection Sergeant Gardner relaxed somewhat, but at any rate, he licked us into shape as well as anyone could have done it.

We were recompensed for all we went through, however, by getting our "final leave" and after we had been handed our tickets and were safely in the train "homeward bound" we felt we had earned the right to look askance at civilians of military age, and this we proceeded to do.

*From the Regimental Magazine*
THE EXPLORER

In the early days of 1915 life in the New Army was full of interest to the new recruit. He was entering upon a new life himself and was meeting in that life an almost infinite variety of character. In some battalions the two extremes of life were thrown together; the wealthy and the poor, the scholarly and the illiterate, the traveller and the untravelled village youth. In other battalions types were much more on a level.

The explorer was in the company of men from all grades of society, but he liked the untravelled and the inexperienced men best, for such men always provided him with an audience when he felt like spinning a yarn – which was pretty often. He had spent many years in West Africa, roaming through the forests, searching for timber, plants, herbs, seeds, or anything else which might be turned into commerce. In his early youth he had been in one of the Hussar regiments as an officer, so he said; but few of his comrades were prepared to believe this. His only proficiency as a soldier consisted in "dodging" parades, and this he did to perfection; one of the few occasions on which he turned out happened to be a day on which company training in "attack" had been ordered.

He started off with plenty of show and bounce. unmindful of the fact that the men on either side of him had repeatedly to push him into place, which is of course contrary to rule, but when it came to doubling in extended order he soon developed the feeling of being fed up, and seeing a hole in the ground to slip his foot into it and rolled over in apparent agony. Ever afterwards he excused himself from such parades by complaining of the injury he had then received. When wanted for a parade, it was found that the company quartermaster sergeant had some clerical work to be done, and out would come some sheets of paper, pen and ink, and he would settle down to write. Needless to say, he had previously told his tale of unfitness to the sergeant and had offered his services in this respect. Strange to say, this kind of thing was allowed to continue.

He was never short of extras in the way of food. His exploring faculties stood him in good respect in this way.

"What! Mushrooms for breakfast, Blank?"

"Yes, mushrooms - I have been out gathering them this morning whilst you lazy bounders were asleep in bed."

"Who cooked them for you?"

"I had them cooked at the cookhouse. I got round the cook-sergeant, and he has offered to do them as often as I like."

In cold weather when the allowance was proved to be inadequate, there was no lack of fire in the stove at his end of the hut.

"Where did you find that wood?"

A strict order had been issued against cutting down hedges for this purpose.

"Found it in the field opposite, to be sure."

"But it has been lopped off a tree. Where did you get the axe?"

"Found it lying about. Those Pioneers are such careless beggars; they never put their tools away."

The truth was he had "sneaked it", and it gave the Pioneers no end of trouble to find it again. Seeing him use a hammer and a steel wedge for splitting up the wood, questions again were asked.

"Where did you get your tools?"

"Found them in the road yonder. The road repairers had left them about."

Those tools were never returned. Nearly every day some such item of interest would crop up, and these things, along with the numerous tales he told, kept us fairly lively.

Amongst the tales he told was one to the effect that he had been offered a commission in one of the native regiments to go and fight against the Germans in the Cameroons. He had replied that he would accept on the condition that he be allowed to go his own way with his troops: and had this been granted, the Germans would have been driven out of that country long before they were, so he said. But his request was not granted. In place of this he was offered the duty of conveying German prisoners to England, which post he had accepted, and that accounted for his presence amongst us.

He had in his possession in the hut a bottle containing some fluid similar in appearance to blue-black ink. With this he was going to make his fortune. He showed us his correspondence with various shipping companies on the subject. This fluid was a preventative of rust, and when applied to ships it would so preserve the steel plates as to save the shipping companies thousands of pounds per year. It was made from some seeds which he had found in Africa. It had been applied to a steel plate, and towed from Africa to New York, whilst another piece had been treated and placed in the bilge water in the bottom of a ship for six months: and on neither of the pieces treated was there any trace of rust to be found. Unfortunately, I happened to smash the bottle, and the fortune was never realised.

After a while these yarns began to be too wonderful to be believed, and we were not slow in letting him see this. He bore it for a time, and then one day he announced the fact that he had changed huts. In other words, he had found a fresh audience, and thus our close association with him ceased. We were not regretful. We passed on our condolences to the men of the other hut, and then left him in peace.

A Fellow Private.
CHRISTMAS, 1917


Christmas! 'Tis here, that season of the year
When men throw off their cloaks of chill reserve
To show their inner selves in words of cheer
And actions kindly, whereby they preserve
The memory of that first Christmas morn,
On which the Angel host proclaimed to them
Who heard: "Lo, unto you a child is born.
Let there be peace on earth, good will to men."
Peace! Peace on earth, while Armageddon rages!
Is this the end for which mankind has striven,
For which mankind has toiled through all the ages,
That this fair earth asunder should be riven?
No, surely no! This age of strife and tears

Is but the purifying of the earth
Within the fire, that, in the future years,
May come a peace of real and lasting worth.
Then, let us hope, shall Christmas be indeed
(As Christmas never was in ages past)
A time when ev'ry trace of strife and greed
Shall turn to peace and kindliness at last.
Then shall all men, with one another meeting,
Stretch forth the hand of sincere friendship: then
While church-bells gaily ring, shall come the greeting
"True peace on earth, goodwill toward all men."

A O Crane.

## SIERRA LEONE

After a couple of days sail the escort left us, the destroyer "High Flyer" then taking the duties over, arriving at Sierra Leone on January 17th. During our stay there our fellows volunteered to coal the ships assisted by coolies and strange to say were only paid the paltry sum of five shillings for the five days' work done, whilst the coolies were being paid double that price, so much for our labour leader. On route we had concerts and boxing tournaments on deck.

## THE WHITE MAN'S GRAVE
*(Magazine article)*

Sierra Leone! You're a wonderful place!
For a sight of you many would crave;
And yet you are not by the white man beloved,
For you are the White Man's Grave.
The coloured man dwells in your mountains and hills
The West African crafty and brave;
But few whites can live in the moisture and heat
That makes you the White Man's Grave.
Yet you are a part of our Empire so vast.
And that great Empire's way you help pave;
And so we forgive you, Sierra Leone.
For being the White Man's Grave.

### CAPE TOWN

We arrived at Cape Town safely after an exciting time, for we not only turned back for two days owing to enemy vessels, but were ordered below owing to the sighting of a strange ship which afterwards proved to be a neutral one. We eventually arrived at Cape Town (South Africa) on February 5th and after a route march through the principle streets were allowed a few hours' freedom.

We were much surprised to find such a nice place and plenty of English people residing there. Fruit and eatables were very plentiful, and we were treated very generously and pleased to get the fruit etc. they provided us with. After a day's sightseeing we started off once more on our journey, that being February 6th, and after a twelve hour journey around the African coast, just as we were putting on good speed, struck a mine and a serious explosion occurred in the fore part of the ship.

We fell in in good order at our boat stations and rafts and waited for further orders. The S.O.S. signals were sent out and the hideous noise of the siren was heart rending, but one and all kept their heads and after someone started singing the old favourites "Tipperary" and "The Long Long Trail" etc. the whole regiment took it up and cheered the splendid work of the crew.

The distress signals were answered by the "Oxfordshire" and the "U Magnus", the former being a hospital ship conveying wounded troops from German East to South Africa. Few of us were any the worse for our adventure. but sea sickness got the better of a few of us (myself included).

We were taken back to Cape Town and then by train to the Military Centre of Wynberg. The procession through that town was a very comical one from the spectators' point of view as some of us were minus our coats and caps and various other clothing, and each carrying a life-belt apiece, reminding one of the realities of war.

*From the Mag.*

Reuters Agency has been asked to announce the following messages with reference to the accident to the *Tyndareus*. From the Naval Commander-in-Chief, Simon's Town, to the Admiralty:

"The behaviour of Battalion - - - - ★ of the Middlesex

Regiment on board the steamship *Tyndareus* after the accident to that ship, there being a large quantity of water on board and the ship apparently sinking by the head in a heavy swell, was most praiseworthy, and equal to the Birkenhead tradition of the British Army on the same spot. It was only due to this that no lives were lost on the boat. The ship was saved by the coolness and perseverance of the captain, officers, engineers and engine room staff".

From the Admiralty to the Naval Commander-in-Chief, Simon's Town: The following has been received from His Majesty the King:

"Please express to the officer commanding the - - - - ★ Battalion of the Middlesex Regiment my admiration of the conduct displayed by all ranks on the occasion of the accident to the *Tyndareus*. In their discipline and courage they worthily upheld the splendid tradition of the Birkenhead, ever cherished in the annals of the British Army.

George, R.1.


★Wartime censorship prevented the publication of the Battalion number.


*Clipping from the Cape Arms newspaper, February 12 1917*
THE GALLANT MIDDLESEX


The - - - - Battalion of the Middlesex Regiment, which narrowly escaped going down in the steamer *Tyndareus* off this coast last week, awoke this morning to find itself famous. The Middlesex Regiment, needless to state, has a tradition behind it.

It has distinguished itself in many historic campaigns, but nothing in its annals redounds more to its credit than the behaviour of officers and men on the occasion signalised by the King's message of congratulation. The steamer *Tyndareus* was about to call at Table Bay for fuel and supplies, the weather was fine, and the majority of the soldiers were watching another "transport" which was coming behind, when suddenly a terrific shock was felt and the vessel began to fill with water at a great rate. It was a critical moment for everyone on board. Panic or confusion would have resulted in a terrible disaster. But the men, from the highest to the lowest on board, behaved like heroes. All must have realized their danger. Indeed they could not fail to do so, for the steamer could be seen to be going down by the head and threatening to take the final plunge at any moment.

The men responded to the commands of their officers as briskly and as orderly as on parade, and quietly lined up. With death apparently staring them in the face, they burst into song and cheered each other by joining in popular tunes. Boats were loaded quietly and carefully, and with the arrival of assistance all were got off, down to the favourite dogs. It was a magnificent exhibition of coolness and worthy of the highest traditions not merely of the British Army, but also of the British Maritime Service, for it must not be overlooked that the captain, officers and seamen of the steamer displayed equal coolness and were under equally fine discipline.

His Majesty King George, in his message of congratulations to the gallant Middlesex, compares the officers and men's conduct on board the Tyndareus after the accident with the behaviour of the heroes of the *Birkenhead*, whose exceptional coolness and bravery when that vessel met with her fatal accident aroused the enthusiasm of the whole civilised world, and caused the King of Prussia to have an account of the accident read to his troops on parade as an example of splendid courage and discipline.

There is a curious similarity between the two disasters. The *Birkenhead* was also rounding this coast and was in proximity to Cape L'Agulhas when she struck a reef. At once the ship began to fill. The soldiers and sailors, taken by surprise and realizing the danger facing them, sprang to attention at the word of command as though on land and in safety. There was no confusion, no panic. The *Birkenhead*, like the *Tyndareus,* went down at the head and a well-known picture painted from the facts supplied by an eye witness showed her with her stern out of the water, just as the *Tyndareus* is reported to have been at one time. The great and gratifying difference between the two disasters was that those on board the *Tyndareus* were saved and the ship was towed into port in a sinking condition, whilst the majority of those on board the *Birkenhead* went down.

They stood to attention in orderly ranks until the last, some say watching with a grim smile, the sharks swimming around, and their deaths like the brave men they were, without flinching. The loss of life was heavy, the military loss being 358 and the naval loss 87, but the story of that tragedy stands today as one of the grandest examples of bravery on record, and it is held in honour by the Navy as well as the Army of Great Britain.

And the coolness and discipline displayed by the officers and men of the *Tyndareus* have shown that the spirit which held the men of the Birkenhead together still survives. A fact which adds lustre to the incident is that the men of the Middlesex Battalion were not old and seasoned soldiers. They were many of them, at all events, young men fresh from civilian life. That they should have become so quickly impregnated with the high tradition of the British Army and of the distinguished regiment to which they belong is a wonderful proof of the great qualities of the British race.

*From the Mag.*
Should We Smile?
by W. Quaife Collins.

The thing that goes the farthest toward making life worthwhile,
That costs the least and does the most, is just a pleasant smile.
The smile that bubbles from the heart that loves its fellow-men
Will drive away the cloud of gloom and coax the sun again:
It's full of worth and goodness too, with manly kindness blent
It's worth a million dollars, and it doesn't cost a cent.
There is no room for sadness when we see a cheery smile –
It always has the same good luck, it's never out of style:
It nerves us on to try again when failure makes us blue –
Such dimples of encouragement are good for me and you.
So smile away, folks understand what by a smile is meant –
It's worth a million dollars, and it doesn't cost a cent.

## WYNBERG

During our stay there we were entertained by the Mayor and officials at their town hall, a spacious and fine building. We were also presented with memento cards with the King's message on one side, and the address by the citizens of Wynberg on the other. Our time for departing was all too quick as it was the time of our lives.

We played the pick of the Cape Colony at football and after affecting a draw of one all at half time, we suffered defeat by the margin of seven goals to one. We also formed the guard of honour for the opening of the South African Parliament which was performed in state, when photographs were taken and sent to all home newspapers. Rickshaw rides were fine and were pulled by hefty natives.

We were also inspected by His Excellency the Governor General of the Union of South Africa, Lord Buxton.

*Magazine article*
Wynberg Camp
by Gilbert S. Watts, L. Cpl.

Wynberg Camp has a fascination for the men of the 25th. Middlesex Regiment, which has never lost its grip upon them. In imagination we can see it yet: a city of tents built upon the sand and overshadowed by the pines, and towering overhead a few miles away, the beautiful grey cliffs of Table Mountain. In the daytime hot dry sunshine, which never seemed to over-fatigue us, and in the evening and night a delightful atmosphere which reminded us of early English spring weather. It was a camp where in spite of numerous fatigues, men were happy.

There were many and differing kinds of elements about the camp which conspired to make us comfortable and to keep us in high spirits. In various parts were to be seen natives with barrows - drawn mostly by donkeys - upon which were placed for sale a plentiful supply of grapes and other fruits, and at very cheap rates. There were also two separate Institutes where we could buy refreshments and things useful, write our letters and sing our songs and generally make ourselves at home.

The food in the camp supplied by the "Military" was "top-hole" for a tropical climate. Even now it is a common thing to hear men speaking about Wynberg cheese, jam and raisin puddings.

Another feature of interest was to see the A. S. C. Cape Wagons come into the camp, drawn by four and sometimes eight mules and driven by hardy-looking natives with immense whips. It was a sight to do the heart good to see three or four of these wagons laden with grapes, water-melons, etc. - gifts of the South African Comforts Committee - arrive on various mornings outside the quartermaster stores. How we all toiled on fatigues to get the above-mentioned wagons unloaded is another story. There must have been something kindly in the air at Wynberg, for although at all hours of the day men were being collared for fatigues, strange to say they never grumbled overmuch.

The town of Wynberg which adjoins the camp is one of fine buildings and wide, clean streets. It is also blessed with an excellent tram service, which runs to places even so far distant as Cape Town. The population of Wynberg is composed of English, Dutch and the Kaffir class of people. By train or by tram it was possible by large numbers of us to visit places on the coast of such interest as Simonstown, into whose docks the *Tyndareus* was towed: Muizenburg, where one could partake of the famous and rare surf bathing; Calk Bay, another good spot for bathing; and in the other direction one could go to the noble Cecil Rhodes Memorial at Groote Schuur, Cape Town, and from thence up the side of the Table Mountain by tramcar to the beautiful Camps Bay.

But in spite of the attractions of neighbouring places of interest, most of our time was spent at Wynberg itself, and particularly at the Town Hall. It is impossible to express adequately our feelings of appreciation for all the exceeding great kindness of the Wynberg Mayor and people. Both collectively and individually they did all they could to make us feel absolutely at home at Wynberg. All day long their large and stately Town Hall was open to the troops, where games, reading and writing materials, music, refreshments and tobacco were provided free of all cost! Indeed, on several occasions, notably on our arrival and departure, they gave us extra special concerts and refreshments. In addition they formed parties for picnics and tennis, and hardly one of our number could say that he did not receive at the very least, one personal invitation to spend the evening at one or other of their houses.

When the time came for us to leave our camp and say "Goodbye" to our Wynberg friends, there was not one of us who did not do so with regret. The time we spent in Wynberg Camp is one of our most pleasant recollections, and it is written upon the tablet of our memory forever.

*Newspaper cutting - The Heroes of the Tyndareus.*

## HEADLINE – WARM TRIBUTES AT THE
## WYNBERG COUNCIL. ARRANGEMENTS FOR
## ENTERTAINING THE REGIMENT.

Warm tributes to the men of the Middlesex Regiment, who behaved so gallantly on the *Tyndareus*, were paid at the Municipal Council last night. Major Sydney Cowper said he would like to move a hearty vote of appreciation of the manner in which the officers and men of the Middlesex Regiment and the Captain of the ship behaved. They behaved just like the troops on the "Birkenhead", added Major Cowper, they were men from A to Z. The Mayor said such a motion would have the approval of every member of the council.

Mr. G. S. Withinshaw, M. L. A., thought they must not lose the sight of the fact that the men were here only temporarily and were not able to make regular arrangements. Many of the men had lost their kits, and he thought they would be well advised to endeavour to provide for them in the way the Mayor had suggested.

Mr. T. Ferguson said he would like to see the men charged nothing at all for refreshments. "There are 1,000 of them", he said "and if one cannot provide 1,000 cups or even 10,000 cups of tea after what these fellows have done for us, well we are not Wynbergers at all. I am not wealthy but I will be pleased as a member of the council to do my share." (Hear Hear.) "These men have left their homes, many of them are invalids and are going to do the best that they can for their country, and I say that we, who are sitting quietly here, knowing very little about the war, should do the best that we can for them" (Hear Hear).

Mr. T. Millward said they were all agreed that they must do the best they could for these men. Few knew of what had been done for them in the Town Hall on Friday and Saturday night. On Friday night something like 1300 or 1400 cups of tea and coffee, together with buns and cigarettes, had been provided, and on Saturday night 1500 teas were served. He thought that this spoke well for Wynberg (Hear Hear.) Many of the residents knew nothing at all about it, and he was sure that they would be prepared to put their hands in their pockets. If money was wanted on an occasion like this they had only to ask for it (Hear Hear.)

Mrs Duncan Taylor thought that they should leave themselves in the hands of the ladies in this matter. They had many ladies in Wynberg who were experts at this kind of work, and with the backing of the council they should be allowed to make their own arrangements. "I think" added Mrs Taylor, "we may congratulate the Mayor on the spontaneous entertainments given on Friday and Saturday nights. It was good to see these poor fellows, after what they had done, enjoying themselves. If it had been known, the Wynberg people would have crowded the hall."

The Mayor said if it was the wish of the council that the use of the Town Hall and free refreshments should be granted, he was quite willing.

Mrs Duncan Taylor said that there was a limit to the amount of work which the ladies were able to do. He thought they should consult them on the matter first.

It was decided to grant the use of the Town Hall and Reading Room, from 3 pm to 9.30 pm from today, and free refreshments, the arrangements being left in the hands of the Mayor and the ladies of Wynberg.

Mr. Cowper's motion was also adopted, and the town clerk was instructed to convey the resolution by letter to the officer commanding the regiment.

## AN OFFICER'S TRIBUTE TO TROOPS' BRAVERY.

At an intercession service in the Wynberg Town Hall yesterday afternoon, Lt. Sylvester Lee, of the Middlesex Regiment, paid a tribute to the bravery of the troops during the recent accident to the Tyndareus as follows:

The other night when we stood on the deck of the Tyndareus immediately after the accident, our colonel stood upon the bridge and spoke to the men who were nearest. He said, "Men of the 25th. This is your hour in which you are to be tested. We all ought to have lived for this hour all of our lives. Obey orders and we may be able to save you, let us die like Englishmen (Cheers). "We who are the officers of the 25th," cautioned Lieut. Lee, "are I think rightly proud of our men, and their performance on this occasion" (Cheers). But I will tell you a little secret. Day by day we used to assemble there alongside the boats so that every man would know where his place was in case of accident, and some of us said, "I wonder what sort of performance it will be if there is an accident". We had our doubts about it, and when the occasion came it proved that underneath an apparently careless exterior was all the power to stand still and not murmur even in the face of death" (Cheers).

MISSIONARY TO SOLDIER.
ADDRESS BY OFFICER OR GALLANT REGIMENT.
ARTICLE PRINTED IN CAPE ARMS NEWSPAPER.

An interesting address was given at the service of intercession held in the Wynberg Town Hall yesterday afternoon by Lieut. Sylvester Lee, of the Middlesex Regiment. There was a crowded gathering, among whom were a great many men in khaki.

"I had better begin perhaps" said Lieut. Lee, 'by telling you a bit of my own experience so far as my present situation is concerned. This war has brought into existence so many strange things. Men are finding themselves in positions which at one time they never thought they would fill, and I am one of these men. After being engaged for many years as a preacher and a missionary, and hating the very thought of war, at the call of duty I enlisted more than two years ago as a private (cheers).

"It seems a strange beginning, having laid aside, as it were, the teaching of peace and taken up the bayonet and the rifle and tried to understand how to use them, and even to the extent of learning how to throw bombs. I am only one among tens of thousands whose lives have been completely changed by the present war, but having been a preacher and having tried to understand human nature before the war, my thoughts have been particularly turned upon the one subject of the human soul.

I myself have never been at the front, being considered an old man and not fit to go. I have been at the point of going twice, but I have had to be content with hearing what goes on at the front.

First of all, I want to say that this war has revealed human nature in many of its aspects, human nature as we had almost ceased to think of it before the war. It has brought to light the defects and the virtues of the human soul."

Lieut. Lee referred to some of the defects which had been revealed, but pointed out on the other hand, how the war had developed countless instances of heroism, self-sacrifice and devotion to duty. It had been said that society in general had been given up to the lust of pleasure, that men and women were becoming pampered, were becoming selfish in their pleasures and were rolling in luxury, until the power of self-sacrifice and of noble deeds seemed to have been lost.

But this war has shown that down in the human heart there were noble powers, which only awaited the condition to bring them forth. He thought we could be proud of our manhood, which had been willing to give up so much in the way of self-sacrifice during the present war.

One matter with which Lieut. Lee had, he remarked, been struck was the fatalism which seemed to exist to a very considerable extent in the British Army. He had known previously that it existed in individuals, but he had been surprised that it existed among so many. Their attitude was that God had appointed the length of life and the manner of death, and he must say that in some cases it had proved of service to the man in the hour of need, for many a man had gone over the top, meeting the foe with a sort of recklessness in his breast, in that he thought, "If I am to be killed, I shall be killed. If I am to be saved, I shall be saved. At any rate I will do my best".

Mr J. McDonald (Mayor of Wynberg) presided. The devotional exercises were led ag the Rev. O. M. Watters and E.

W. Lasbrey, and a portion of scripture was read by the Rev. H. A. Lewty. Mrs Webb Richards, with much acceptance, read "O Rest in the Lord". The hymns were accompanied by the band of the Middlesex Regiment. The collection is to be devoted to the cause for entertaining visiting troops in Wynberg.

## DURBAN

We left Cape Town on February 26th. and boarded the "lngoma" and left port at six o'clock that evening. We arrived at the beautiful town of Durban on March 2nd. and paraded through the principal streets, finishing up at the pretty park where the officials of that town were gathered to welcome us, and after a few speeches to which Colonel John Ward responded, we did justice to a fine spread of eatables that was prepared for us. After that ceremony was over we had our liberty, some accepting the hospitality of the local residents, others took advantage of the local tramway which charged us nothing to ride upon. There was a race meeting proceeding and taking all things into consideration our two days at Durban were well spent.

*From the Regimental Magazine*
## DURBAN

Durban is the name of another South African town which has captured for itself a place in the hearts of the men of the 25th Middlesex Regiment. Durban was our first port of call after leaving Cape Town, and we arrived there on Friday, March 2nd, at seven o'clock in the morning, after a journey lasting only four days. As we entered the fine harbour, with its floating and graving docks, and viewed the attractive beach and town, the question upon everyone's lips was: "Shall we be allowed to go ashore?" Our Colonel did not disappoint us, and within two hours of our arrival at the quayside, a very cheerful body of men were marching through the streets of Durban. The people of Durban had made every arrangement to give us a royal reception. Their own band, playing lively airs, accompanied us through the streets lined with enthusiastic cheering crowds until we reached the Albert Park, where we received a public welcome to the borough. The Mayor of Durban, on behalf of himself and burgesses, made a hearty and choice speech of welcome, to which our Colonel replied. Afterwards we were served with excellent refreshments and cigarettes by the ladies, and then we spent the remainder of the day seeing the sights.

Durban is perhaps the prettiest and most British town in South Africa. It's well laid-out streets, big business houses, magnificent harbour, great expanse of ocean beach and avenues of suburban villas stamp it out as a city of no mean order. One of the sights of the place was to see big strong Zulus running about in curious native costume with rickshas.

Some of the statistics which indicate the public work carried out in Durban are worthy of mention. There are one hundred miles of roads bearing thirty-five miles of electric tramways that carry a million souls per month. Electric lamps to the number of two thousand and sixty-two illuminate the streets, and there are over six thousand one hundred and fifty-two private consumers of electric light. There is no lack of excellent water, and the sewage system is all that could be desired.

During the course of the two days we spent there we discovered to our joy that Durban, in spite of the shark-infested waters, offers good facilities for surf bathing, and an open-air bath which is reported to be the largest of its kind in the world. We were also very pleased to find that the Mayor and Corporation had kindly given permission for us to use the cars free of cost whenever we liked. Needless to say, we took full advantage of such kindness and thereby were able to see all round, not only the beautiful town, but some of the surrounding district. We noted many well- built and stately buildings, but have only the space to mention the names of a few: the Town Hall, Municipal Art Gallery, General Post Office and Law Courts. Dotted here and there all over the town were places of entertainment for the troops, which were much used and greatly appreciated. Some of our number enjoyed pleasant walks, seeing therefore such centres of interest as the Botanical Gardens, Lord's (Cricket) ground and the Race Course. One of the members of our battalion describes how he walked out into the country as far as Umbilo, going on the way through Banana Plantations and Orange Groves and had a chat with the Hindoo owner thereof.

Altogether our brief stay in Durban proved to be a thoroughly enjoyable time. The people were kindness personified and some of us made friendships which will remain unbroken until long after the war is over. Our only hope is that some time in the future many of us may be allowed to re-visit a town of such fascinating interest and charm which is inhabited by a people of such unusual kindly spirit.

*From the Mag.*
SOUTH AFRICA

A dominion of Britain's great Empire,
And a land that is second to none,
With a climate well-nigh idealistic –
That's South Africa, land of the sun

It has cost us an ocean of treasure,
Seas of blood shed as freely as rain.
Isandhlwana, Spion Kop, Magersfontein –
These are names we remember with pain.

But it's worth all that blood and that treasure;
It's a prize that is worth fighting for.
There's no need to seek El Dorado;
It is found and is ours evermore.

Tis a vision of wild, savage beauty,
With its Kopjes and Dongas and Kloofs
With its spruits, and its drifts, and the great veld,
And its farmhouses white, with red roofs.

Can you picture its groves and plantations
With their trees and their flowers and fruit?
Can you picture its sheep and its oxen,
And the big game that men love to shoot?

Can you picture the gold and the diamonds,
Which are found in its numerous mines?
Can you picture those Zuid Afrikanders,
And the native kraals, built up in line?

Ah! South Africa's truly delightful,
My hope is to see it again;
For I spent my life's happiest moments
On a dusty South African plain.

May the Union of Dutchman and Briton
Into one great South African race
Be soon firmly, effectually welded,
Past dissensions at length to efface.

– O. Crane (9-3-17)

## INDIAN OCEAN

We started our last lap on March 4th, at 7 am, mid the farewell of a good crowd. We crossed the equator on March 12th and Friday March 16th was an exciting day for we were told to be ready and we were forbidden to strike matches or smoke on the decks.

Saturday 17th: Burial of a "C" company lad attended by all, several deaths having occurred on other ships, especially the "Empress of Britain", which had several hundred troops down through inoculations.

March 20th, alarm sounded and all were ordered down

below. March 22: entered the straits of Malacca when we encountered a monsoon and were pulled up by a patrolling destroyer, HMS Fame, and on March 23 pilots came aboard and examined papers of ship.

*From the Magazine*
OUR LOSS

We desire to keep in memory the names of those who have been taken from us by death, and to record our sympathy to their relatives and friends. Private H. Quickenden passed away on the 15th March and was buried at sea at three pm on the 17th. The burial service was conducted by Lieut. S. Lee, Wesleyan Methodist minister.

THE ARK
"THAT INGOMA"

When I remember wretched Noah
How safely in the Ark he bore
Two of each kind of living thing,
Of beasts that howl, and birds that sing
The insects too that crawl and creep
And sting poor fellows in their sleep

It seems to me that on this Bark,
The floating zoo, nicknamed the Ark,
He must have, in some trance or coma,
Had visions of the old Ingoma,

And feebly tried to imitate
Her living crew both small and great.

Upon this ship you saw no lions.
Doubtless they were below in irons:
I know we had some mournful "Gnus"
Which promptly gave us all the blues,
When raiders were to sink us bound,
The "Gee Gees" they would trumpet round,

And, tho' tis hard such words to pass,
On board was many a "blooming ass",
And if you disbelieve, I'll wager
You need to ask the Sergeant-Major;
"For some were donkeys. some were fools,
And others obstinate as mules!"

And 'tween the decks drawn up close column
Were beetles big, and small and solemn:
Cockroaches brown and very horrid,
At night they drilled upon your forehead.
And many another insect pest
Nightly entrenched upon your chest.

And, O! in porridge, or in rice,
That on the surface looked so nice,
You found within its thick interior
Some maggots fine, some quite inferior.
And then would you would with wrathful clatter
Sternly refuse the sticky matter.

Ah! Noah, upon your ancient craft
You with the gay hyenas laugh
Of Noah in pain upon the Ark
I've never heard the last remark;
I who can't live on food's aroma
Found "noring" pains on the Ingoma.

R. B. CRABB.

Little fleas have lesser fleas
Upon their backs to bite them,
And lesser fleas have smaller fleas,
And so, ad infinitum.

SINGAPORE.

We passed a range of pretty islands and arrived at the port of Singapore on the 24th March. It was a great surprise to hear that two companies were to stay here, as not a thought had been given in that direction - Hong Kong we estimated our destination.

It was finally arranged that "A" and "D" companies should stay and the remaining two companies proceed to Hong Kong. We learned that we were replacing an A1 battalion of the Shropshire Light Infantry, who left us a fortnight later for France.

During our sixteen months' stay at Singapore we had a variety of sports but football of course was the king of them all. We played all the local teams at football, and cricket and hockey, and in all the departments, met with success.

We met a Medical Board and one hundred and thirty two were passed A1 and they proceeded to Lucknow, India, where they all got graded B.1. again!

*Magazine Article*
FROM SOMEWHERE IN THE CHINA SEA
BY L. CPL. H. MACALLISTER

Have you ever found yourself in that perfect state where peace, perfect peace pervades all, and it is almost too much trouble to get up for meals? That's a state I am gliding into; but I manage to overcome the very strong inclination to remain in that state of coma into which most of us are drifting when I hear the old gong go for meals. I have never thought a great deal of the gong as a musical instrument, and don't even now by itself; but when you know that it is the tocsin which calls one and all to a rattling meal you have simply got to respect it.

Gastronomy is not one of my strong points. I am not able to run over the menu of a dinner the day after and to give full details of each course, with a look on my face like the girl in the picture "The Soul's Awakening." I eat, but finish there.

I hope nobody will think I am taking a rise out of the grub. I am not. Even as I write these lines the appetising small of hot coffee and bacon is wafted towards me. The vessel is travelling as smoothly as a tube train: there is plenty of room for everybody, and I haven't heard a wicked word since we came on board.

We have nothing to do with the "washing up" after meals. There are Chinese to do all that. They wait at table and do everything. The heat is gradually increasing, and with it there is a decreasing desire to do anything at all. There are some 500 Chinese on board, and just now they are undergoing their bi-weekly medical examination.

By the way, some one or two had the "wind up" the day we left. I am rather handicapped in telling this narrative, as I don't wish to mention any names and so give offence. We were all sitting below - or, rather, those of us able to sit up, the rest being on their backs very, very sick. The vessel was steaming merrily onwards, doing a nice twelve knots. For my own part, I with three others, was engaged in a quiet game of solo whist when the incident happened. We most of us remember the evening on the 6th of February of last year, with the sea a sheet of burnished gold, when we "got it in the neck." We laugh and joke about that night now, but at the time we really had the "wind up" somewhat.

The evening I am writing about was just such another. Everything was nice and peaceful, and submarines and mines were far from our thoughts. One of our little party had just called "Abundance" when a loud report was heard on deck, and there was a rush of steam - just such a sound as haunted us on the night made famous by us. A rush was made for the companionway. I stopped in my place with a view to putting the stakes in a safe place. Faces were blanched and teeth were clenched. We waited as "Die-Hards" should for the vessel to settle down, and we all wished that we had been kinder to our little sisters, and resolved that if we should be spared once more, we would be better men - if possible. I heard a voice near me, and it had quite a pathetic ring in it. "Just my luck! I let old Bill have my ruddy lifebelt, and the perisher is sitting on the foc'sle; I'm done. Good-bye boys! Give my love to them all at home. Good-bye!" We were very relieved that it was only a steam-pipe burst.

We are reaching S - - - - tomorrow eve, and are, I believe, going on shore to T — - - B - - - - on Wednesday. The exercises necessitated by the walk won't do us any harm. As we were paid off soon after we set sail, most of us will have some money to burn. The concert party is going very strong, and there was quite a decent sing-song last Saturday.

I must break off now to catch the mail, but will let you know more of our travels at a later date. Meanwhile, Cheer-ho! to all the Middlesex men we have left behind.

BIRTHDAYS:

November 21st & 26th. We must congratulate our Colonel, who celebrated his entry into the second half-century of birthdays on November 21st. The officers and their wives were kindly entertained to dinner by him. The N.C.O.s and men were also remembered and drank the health of our Colonel, wishing him long life and a continuance of his success of the first half-century.

To Mrs F. J. Browne we also offer over heartiest congratulations on passing her - - th. birthday on November 26th. Major and Mrs Browne entertained the officers, their wives and friends to tea and tennis. By kind permission of Lieut. Col. John Ward, M.P., the Regimental Band was in attendance, and a very enjoyable afternoon was spent.

*Newspaper Article - The Herts Advertiser and St. Albans Times.*
*Soldier's Letters.*
The Scene of the *Tyndareus.*

We have received further letters from soldiers engaged in various parts of the far flung battle area, giving interesting accounts of their work and incidentally expressing their appreciation of the 'Herts Advertiser' and the opportunity which the receipt of it affords them of keeping in touch with local affairs.

Private Alfred Arthur Bridges, of the Middlesex Regiment, whose home is at 105 Verulam Road, St. Albans, who, before the war was a well-known member of the Elstree Athletic Club, representing them in the North London and North of the Thames championship in 1913 and 1914; was also playing secretary for several seasons of the St Albans Thursday Football Club, and before enlisting was employed by Messrs E. Day and Co. of Marlborough Road, St. Albans, writes to us from Singapore:

Having much interest in St. Albans I thought it my duty to write a few lines regarding my adventures on my journey to the Far East. We left Aldershot, our training centre, on December 24th and arrived at Plymouth, where the SS Tyndareus was waiting for us on the following day. We left that port on January 5th and arrived at Sierra Leone on January 17th, departing on January 23rd for Cape Town, which was reached on February 5th. In the afternoon we marched through the principal streets of the town and were accorded a warm reception. After tea we were allowed out until 9.30.

On the following morning we left at six o'clock and after

about twelve hours journey the accident to the *Tyndareus* occurred just as the ship was picking up a good pace. The majority of the fellows were looking at another ship which we were rapidly leaving behind and were not at all conscious of any danger befalling us, and although it gave us a fright for the moment we gathered our wits together and taking our turns to go down deck to get our life belts, we soon fell in at our boat stations and waited for orders.

When the explosion occurred the ship lurched forward, burying her nose well under the water and with the propellers sticking well out of the water the hopes for saving the ship seemed very small; but we still stuck to our posts and trusted to Providence, and to occupy our spare time we sang "The Long Long Trail" and "Take me Back to Dear Old Blighty", etc. After some time the order came to "all change", so we were transferred to the "Oxfordshire" and the "U. Mayus," I myself being on the former.

We arrived back in Cape Town the following morning, and they took us to Wynberg Camp, where we stayed for three weeks to get re-equipped as a lot of our stock and belongings got lost.

The ship was towed into Simons Town dock in a sinking condition by two cruisers, after being left for lost on the morning following the accident. We left Wynberg on February 26 after the time of our lives in South Africa. The inhabitants gave us concerts and free "feeds" etc., plenty of fruit and cigarettes and before leaving presented us with a copy of the King's message to us regarding the pluck and courage of our lads. The message was - "Please express to the Officer Commanding the 25th Battalion, Middlesex Regiment my admiration of the conduct displayed by all ranks on the occasion of the accident of the *Tyndareus*. In their discipline and courage they worthily upheld the splendid tradition of the Birkenhead, ever cherished in the annals of the British Army. – George R. I.

On the back of this memento was the following message: From the Citizens of Wynbergs - "Town Hall, February 14th. - The citizens of Wynberg are proud to have in their midst the Officers, NCOs and men of the 25th Battalion, Middlesex Regiment and the Mayor and Councillors of the Municipal Council of Wynberg reproduce with all good wishes the message of His Majesty the King as a memento of the bravery exhibited in the accident of the Tyndareus off cape L'Agulhas on February 26 1917". In the top right hand corner are the colours of the battalion with the badge, and in the bottom left hand corner the Arms of the City of Wynberg. At the opening of the South African Parliament by Lord Buxton our Battalion provided the guard of honour and also lined the approach to the Parliament buildings, and the people of Cape Town, having got the wind of our presence, flocked in the main streets to get a good look at our Colonel John Ward, MP, the labour leader and his "gallant men" as the reports in the papers describe us.

We arrived on Friday March 2nd at Durban, where the city band and the Mayor and Corporation and ladies were waiting to receive us in their beautiful park and after a sterling speech by the Mayor we did justice to a good spread of food on the cricket ground. Plenty of cigarettes and cigars followed, and, being free for the day, many of us accepted invitations to visit local residents. Our two-day stay was soon over and we once again moved out of port on the last lap which took us nineteen days to cover. It was a good voyage during that time, and the eastern sunsets looked lovely and worth photographing, for it is a splendid sight to see. In conclusion I may state we are having a good time at this station but there is nothing that beats dear old England.

I must apologise for taking so much of your valuable space, but the Herts paper goes round the room, for there is a Redbourn chap and several Luton fellows who soon worry when they know the "St. Albans Times" is about.

## CONDOLENCE.

We offer our heartfelt sympathy to Pte. T. H. De Neut, of "D" Coy., Singapore, on the death of his wife. Such a loss when thus separated is doubly hard to bear.

## SINGAPORE.

In the last month's edition of "The Mag" we outlined an account of our visit to Durban. Our next port of call after many weeks of anxious journeying was Singapore. Singapore is an island situated off the southern extremity of the Malay Peninsula, and is about twenty-seven miles in length and fourteen miles in breadth. It is one of the greatest ports in the world, being a port for vessels trading Europe or India and the Far East, the North of Australia and the Netherland Indies. The climate is almost uniform throughout the year, and on the whole Europeans find it fairly healthy.

We hailed our arrival at Singapore with unspeakable delight, but the news that half the battalion was to be left behind to garrison the Colony had the effect of partially turning our joy into mourning. As soon as our boat touched the quayside an army of enterprising Chinese appeared in sight carrying loads of stuff to sell to the troops. Among other of their wares they had innumerable boxes of cigars and every other description of tobacco. Needless to say that before the day closed many a Chinaman went away with a light basket and a heavy pocket, and likewise the soldiers were happy in the possession of much needed luxuries.

The day of our arrival was the twenty-third of March. and we spent altogether a very busy two days before the ship again set sail.

"A" and "D" had to reluctantly get all their possessions together and leave the ship on the afternoon of the day we arrived. We were all very unwilling to part company, but had no choice or say in the matter. Major Guest was left in charge of the detachment.

In the evening of the next day, March 24th, "B" and "C" companies were taken for a route march through part of the town. Owing to the fact that our way took us mostly through the native quarters, we were by no means charmed by what we saw and when we were once more on board ship we all felt very thankful that after all our destination was Hong Kong.

Further on in the town were to be seen a large number of fine buildings, but on the whole we were not favourably impressed with Singapore. However we were all glad to have had the privilege of making even so slight an acquaintance with a colony of such fame and power. We are all looking forward to seeing Singapore again, but only that we may then pick up our comrades, as we journey back to dear old "Blighty" on board the Tyndareus - perhaps!

*From the Mag.*
LIFE ON THE INGOMA

*As sung to large audiences on the hatchtops while crossing*
*the Indian Ocean*

We are but soldiers mild and meek
Our pay is just three bob a week:
The more we do, the more we may -
It makes no difference to our pay.

Our trip to China, while it lasts,
Is oft composed of daily fasts,
For maggots fat and maggots lean
Are often in our porridge seen

Our bakehouse should be full of bread -
It's full of cockroaches instead;
And when they're tired and get the hump,
Into our bread they quickly jump.

When orderly sergeants do pass by,
"Men for fatigues" they loudly cry:
And when the privates see their book
They very quickly take their hook.

At 8 o'clock tis breakfast time,
And then we all sit down to dine:
And when we've finished our good blow,
We all line up for the M.O.

Whatever ailments we possess
From broken legs to costiveness,
The doctor says "Ah! now I'll shine
Just give this man a No. 9!"

Inspection time is half-past ten.
The orderly men are busy till then!
And then you'll hear some mother's son
Loudly blowing, "Here they come!"

The Grand March Past has now begun.
It's to attention everyone:
And when they've gone, an awful wail,
As the orderlies sing the "Long Lost Trail".

Then once again comes feeding time
Again we all sit down to dine,
A ten-course dinner - what a treat!
New teeth required to eat the meat!

Our correspondence next we do -
Writing to Maudie, Jane or Sue;
But after writing pages nine
The censor kindly leaves a line.

Then after tea, a terrible rush
Out on deck to avoid the crush.
Swinging our hammocks everywhere,
For down below you get no air.

A diary of our daily work,
Which proves we have no time to shirk
And only goes to show the way
That we spend life on a tanner a day.

L. Corpl. Philby & Pte Melbourne


*From the Regimental Magazine.*
Three Months at Tanglin Barracks.
by L. Corp. R. A. Theobald, B. A.


The order for "A" and "D" Companies to prepare for landing at Singapore came as a complete surprise, at any rate to the rank and file of the "Mine-Dodgers." In the confusion and bustle of the few hours which followed the receipt of the order, we were too busy, and incidentally too "sweaty," to bother about diagnosing our feelings in the matter. Had we done so, we should probably have found mingled satisfaction and disappointment – satisfaction that the long, monotonous voyage was over, and that we were to bid farewell to the luxurious and spacious quarters (save the mark!) which we had been enjoying on the "Ingoma"; disappointment that we were not to see Hong Kong, a place which somehow seems to suggest greater possibilities in the way of romantic scenes, strange customs, etc., than Singapore.

Visions of our departure from Aldershot and Wynberg, loaded with kit bags, equipment, rifles, blankets, etc., with a long, long, trail of perspiring stragglers bringing up the rear, were happily dispelled by the appearance of transport wagons, so that although we found the march up to the barracks quite warm enough to be pleasant, we had a chance to look round us at the quaint Chinese and Malay villages near the docks, and at the beautiful villas in the neighbourhood of the barracks.

Life at Tanglin is by no means unpleasant, although it is bound to be somewhat monotonous. The bungalows, each accommodating 100 men, are lofty and airy, and delightfully cool even in the middle of the day. Shortly after our arrival we were served out with pyjamas, and sheets are used instead of blankets, so that sleeping conditions are quite good.

The mosquito nets, of course, were strange at first. The study of insect life proved a most diverting pastime on the "Ingoma", but there it was confined chiefly to meal-times. Here the ubiquitous cockroach of the troop-deck finds his way into our stew, puddings and bread; but even he was a gentleman compared with the mosquito. The genius of these little creatures for finding an opening in a badly-tucked-in net is astounding. After "Lights out" one can often see a shadowy form dimly outlined in a neighbouring net, matches are struck, and frantic dabs made here and there until a sotto voce, "Got you at last, you little - - - !" announces the fate of the intruder.

Before settling down to work, we were inspected on the Friday after our arrival by the G.O.C., Major-General Ridout, and on the following day by H. E. the Governor, Sir Arthur Young. On both occasions a cordial welcome to Singapore was extended to the battalion, especially to those officers and men who had seen active service in France and elsewhere during the War.

Work, of course, is confined to the earlier part of the day, with an occasional evening parade as an "extra". Even before the heat is trying, and one can see Private X -, wounded at the Marne, coming in after a CO's parade- perhaps company and battalion drill, perhaps a brilliantly planned and more or less perfectly executed attack on some important strategic point in or near the barracks – and sighing, as he wrings out his dripping shirt and puts on a dry one, for the comparative peace and quiet of the trenches. Parades are always done in shirt sleeves, with one exception - church parade.

The church is so cool and shady that chronic sufferers from ecclesiastical beriberi should have no difficulty in keeping their attentions on the service, especially as conducted by our popular "padre".

During the heat of the day a siesta is the general rule, although sundry energetic spirits make afternoon excursions into the so-called "jungle" near the barracks, and return laden with coconuts and pine-apples which form a welcome addition to the Army diet.

We have plenty of opportunities for sport - football, hockey, swimming, gymnastics etc - but another writer is dealing with this subject, unfortunately it gets dark soon after six o'clock, and the passing of the rest of the evening in a pleasant and profitable manner is still a problem with many. On two occasions we have been entertained to concerts in town. The first was the farewell concert to the Shropshires, the second a performance by the well-known conjurer and illusionist Chung Ling Soo. Both entertainments were held in the Victoria Hall, and were thoroughly enjoyed by all present.

Our own "gaff" has been the scene of two concerts: one given by our own fellows and the Shropshires on the evening before the departure of the latter, the other by a travelling concert party, the three juvenile members of which were decidedly clever, both as comediennes and contortionists.

The church room is always well filled in the evening, and should be even better patronised now that the whole building is lit up. Second Lieut. Treacher conducts a weekly Bible class and a short service on alternate Sunday evenings. Bagatelle, cards, ping-pong and other indoor games, magazines, books etc., are provided for the men, and are much appreciated.

The whist-drives are very popular, and it is hoped that it may be possible to arrange a series of lectures, debates, concerts etc, which will not only relieve the monotony, but will be helpful to those men who take part in the entertainments, as well as to those who listen.

The town itself, after the first novelty has worn off, has few attractions for the majority. Perhaps the chief thing one notices is the tremendous mixture of races; Malays, Chinese, Tamils, Japanese, Klings, etc, crowd the streets and shops in European costume to a loin cloth and a smile. One is struck too by the almost complete absence of horses. The European residents and the wealthy natives all appear to use motor cars, while the less fortunate have to be content with a ricksha. It is most amusing to wander down the streets for the first time, glancing in at the shops, most of which are quite open. In one a carpenter is busy making furniture; next door a Japanese dentist, with apparently most up-to-date apparatus, is struggling with a refractory molar; then piles of snow-white linen mark a Chinese laundry - and so on until every conceivable trade is represented. Unlike the coolies, who never seem to exert themselves in the slightest, the tradespeople of the town are at work from early in the morning till late at night.

It is unfortunate that the town is so far away, as we are unable to take full advantage of the splendid efforts of the Y.M.C.A. on our behalf. Their premises are always at the disposal of the troops, and for the past few weeks Saturday evening concerts have been arranged, and on the whole well supported.

Life here is pretty much what we make it. It is up to every man to keep himself as fit as possible, so that when "the first ten years" of which Sergeant Major Gordon was so fond of talking are over, we may prepare for our return to Blighty and civilian life with the feeling that "things might have been a good deal worse."

## CONGRATULATIONS.

A recent mail brought good news to Sergt. Hunting and to Corpl. Chifney. Sergt. Hunting is now the richer by the arrival of a baby daughter, and Corpl Chifney by the arrival of a son. All are doing well.

## BEFORE IT IS TOO LATE

If you've a grey-haired mother
In the old home far away;
Sit down and write the letter
You put off day by day.
Don't wait until her tired steps
Reach Heaven's pearly gates
But show her what you think of her
Before it is too late.
If you've a tender message
Or a loving word to say,
Don't wait till you forget it,
But write to her today.
Who knows what bitter memories
May haunt you if you wait?
So make your loved ones happy
Before it is too late.
We live but in the present,
The future is unknown:
Tomorrow is a mystery,
Today is all our own,
The chance that fortune lends to us
May vanish while you wait,
So spend your life's rich pleasure
Before it is too late.

The tender words unspoken,
The letters never sent,

The long-forgotten messages,
The wealth of love unspent,
For these some hearts are breaking,
For these some loved ones wait –
So show them that you care for them
Before it is too late.

W. Quaif Collins.

*From the Mag.*
Tommy on Mosquito Nets
By L. Corpl. R. Green.

Having the good fortune while at Aldershot to meet some soldiers recently returned from Hong Kong, we were assured that a cordial welcome awaited us, especially by mosquitos, centipedes, lizards, scorpions, and sandflies; also another insect not generally mentioned in refined circles. The former have not yet given us a general reception, only a few having left their cards, but the latter we seem to scent, as it were, waiting in the offing in considerable numbers for a favourable opportunity to make our acquaintance. Having drawn our blankets and bedding, we were given two pieces of wood and some muslin. The wood at first we thought were chopsticks, and the muslin a summer garment. Later we discovered it was an apparatus for hanging over our beds; its alleged purpose being to keep away mosquitos while enjoying a well-earned repose.

After a little jig-sawing the pieces of wood are put together like a cross, to which the muslin is tied. Tape not being an essential of masculine apparel, the nets are tied on in all shapes. the centre tape being invariably connected up with the end of the stick. The next thing is to hang it over the bed on a hook pendant from the ceiling . You stand on the bed and try to put it on the hook, finding yourself on the floor with the net about you like a snake and the wood on your head. The next time you cannon your head against the iron rack over the bed.

The net having been made fast, the first night or two you let the net hang loosely to the ground. But the mosquito is not so easily cheated of his prey: he manages to find a way up underneath, and having had his bite tries to depart. Not finding an exit so easily, he keeps up a perpetual buzz, all efforts to dislodge him proving unavailing. One soon learns that the best way to keep them out is to tuck the net in all round. If you see a Tommy on his back under a bed, throwing his arms and feet in the air, do not imagine he is in a fit: he is only trying to tuck his net up so he will not tear it. When he has retired with his net hanging all around him, he gives one the impression of a joint of meat in a safe or a wild animal encaged for the protection of a long-suffering public.

But it is while on the Taihowan Guard one sees the mosquito net at its best. Three boards are supported by wooden trestles, on which Tommie tries to get a little rest. Above is a loose wire on which, after a few acrobatic feats, he manages to tie his net. Lying on the boards it is a matter requiring considerable dexterity to draw the net around one. Trying to move without disturbing the net results in the trestles moving apart, the occupant of the boards finding himself on the floor, so one remains rigid, being stiff and sore as the outcome. Toiling slowly up the hill in the morning, Tommie is of the opinion that sleeping on boards in a mosquito-infected hut, with a curtain, should be one of the tortures meted out to the person responsible for this worldwide conflagration.

## GUARDS OF HONOUR

On the 4th August 100 NCOs and men of the Middlesex Regiment formed a Guard of Honour under Captain Thomas and 2nd. Lieut. Bouckley: the occasion was the attendance of the Governor at the mass meeting of the Singaporeans held in the Victoria Hall on the anniversary of the declaration of war. The men were justly complimented by the Governor. On the 10th September another guard of NCOs and men were chosen for Government House on the occasion of the visit of the Prince of Siam to Singapore; this guard was in charge of Captain Knowles and 2nd Lieut. Treacher, and was also complimented on its smart turnout, the Prince evincing a knowledge of military matters, as shown by his interest and the questions he asked.

*From the Mag.*
My Reason

With war's stern arms I oft parade,
For England Home and Beauty?
Nay! more the guard room to evade
Than at the call of duty.

I hear no voice, no loving voice,

But one I needs must mention
That sadly fails to me rejoice,
But calls for strict "Attention."

It is the Sergeant Major's shout
It echoes down the breeze,
And having called you "Idiot! Lout!"
He bids you "Stand at Ease!"

And much, I fear, each pace I've trod
In drill's routine of sadness,
Is one step to the "Awkward squad,"
The thought fills me with madness.

"Parade at half-past five each night."
Hark! Tis the Sergeant's warning.
In marching order, miscalled light;
Dread words to hear one morning.

In this damned Squad, upon that square,
The Sergeant gets me well set;
O! for the power to send him, where?
To "Blanco!" like my helmet.

To think that once a little child
I heard, it makes me tearful.
Only my mother's accents mild;
My word! The Army's fearful!
My life is one long sorry drag

The reason why I stick it
The hope that I may one day bag
What? Ninepence and my ticket!

R. B. Craggs

*From the Mag.*
A Dedication to the Drummer

I am dedicating these few lines to the drummer, that is the one on duty for the day. I know that although you are known as a drummer, you do not really "drum" much but mainly "bugle". You may drum a lot presently. I know that if it is not you, it is one of your colleagues, who means to drum in earnest, as he practises assiduously, flams, double flams and the roll, with two sticks on any old thing he can lay hold of. Still, as I said before, at present you mainly "bugle". You bugle through the day and through the night, yes even through the night, for it always seems to me only like the middle of the night, when you sound the rousing call the "Reveille". Ah Bugler, how rudely you intrude and break up so many beautiful dreams, by your disturbing influence on that bit of twisted brass, at such an unearthly hour.

However, you compensate later by the blowing of "Come to the Cookhouse Door," which as a rule you hurry over, as I know you want to get there as quickly as anybody else. I do not blame you. Stew, if not palatable, has an attractive smell.

Then come the Parade Calls, which, no doubt, tax the energies of quite a few. For instance, the "Half-hour Dress" has a tendency to make one hurry, and the "Quarter-hour Dress" creates more haste still, and when the "Fall-in" goes I am sure some of them must be on the point of collapsing. Still, that's none of your business. You have to do it. Yours not to make reply - Yours but to blow and - sir! Yes, sigh for them if you feel so disposed.

Then comes the sick call. I am sure that when you sound this call you must put a certain amount of feeling into it for the poor fellows you are ordering forth. When you see them line up looking so pale, weary, worn and sad, then marched off to the M.O., how your poor heart must ache for them!

And then you must get another pang when you sound the call for "C.O's Orderly Room" and thereafter observe the defaulters, if any, marched straight in without even being allowed to wipe their boots on the mat! If they get C. B. then there is more work for you rounding 'em up every hour or so, as the case may be. Again, this must cause you further pangs at the heart, but whether it be for the defaulters or for yourself at having extra work to do, I can only surmise.

Now, when you sound "Letters" how we could dance around you for joy! You know how we look for those letters from "Saucy Sue". This delightful female is requested to send, to every male, per every mail, some of her choicest selections. Let her send a letter often, says I.

On every Friday you have to exercise your capabilities by sounding the "Pay Call." We should all like you the more if you could make a regular job of it, like the Parade Calls, etc., and sound it every day.

I have heard you sound on rare occasions "No Parade to-day." But when you do sound it, it must cause you a certain amount of gratification, by the applause it creates.

The "First Post" I think you should receive a tat for, and the "Last Post" another "tat too"? although not sufficiently hard to put your "Light Out" but to allow you to blow "Lights Out" according to regulations.

I trust you will digest deeply all I have outlined to you in the foregoing, therefore enough said.

L. Cpl. H. C. Slingsby.

*From the Regimental Magazine*
Tommy on Grousing
By Pte. T. R. Green

"Grousing" is a term very dear to the heart of Tommy Atkins. Like the word "swank" it is not to be found in any dictionary, and though it is practically indefinable, everybody seems to know what it means. In civilian life one heard faint murmurs on quarter days when the rate collector called, also one got a slight acquaintance with it in the pursuance of one's vacation; but for the real unadulterated article the Army has no serious competitor. My first experience of it was while waiting to undergo my medical examination. Some of my companions were letting off a little steam on account of having had to wait two days for an interview with the doctor. To grouse at having to wait a few days at the recruiting office for the privilege of joining up seemed to me unreasonable, but I know better now! I have since learned that grousing is part of the system of Army training. At first I fought very hard against it, but, like many others eventually succumbed. When it was wet and we could not get out we groused when it was fine and we had to drill the result was the same. With the approach of Christmas we began to get in good form. The idea of spending Christmas at Aldershot was the limit, and we rose to the occasion. However the day before Christmas Eve we changed our venue, but not our tune. For the first few days on the bosom of Father Neptune things looked black indeed, not a grouse being heard, the majority being unwell, but after a week or so they got their sea legs on and started to grouse as usual. This state of affairs went on until Cape Town was reached, when a little incident happened that stopped it for a few days. But for a few days only! Little matters about the intaking of a peck of sand per diem with your rations while under canvas were quite enough to start a grouse. When we continued our journey we had some cockroaches for companions. During the day we came across patrols and outposts, but at night on the signal given by a cricket one of the men had brought from Wynberg in his kit bag, they advanced in platoons and companies. Many of the men took an affidavit that never more would they grouse once they set foot on dry land. But it was of no avail. It is far easier to get out of the Army than to get out of the habit. As stated above at first I strove to avoid it, but am pleased to say that now I can grouse with the best of them. We are sitting in our rooms, a driving rain and heavy mist outside and drills are suspended. A corporal is getting together a fatigue party; then we rise to the occasion. There seems to be a recognised scale for grousing. For a five minutes' fatigue one is allowed a ten minutes grouse, and so on. Recently we had a Sports Meeting, and things were flat until the chairman invited grousing. Then we grew warm and enthusiastic, and affairs were soon shaped successfully. It is with a certain amount of misgiving one looks forward to the termination of hostilities.

What will become of the choice phrases one keeps on hand ready to use at the first opportunity? Outside the Army they will be useless. Tommy Atkins is a champion grouse, and when he is grousing he is all right and happy. Many will look back on their life in the Army with pleasure, and declare that the period spent in grousing may be counted among the happiest in their existence. If the first number of this magazine evokes a decent grouse, we know we shall have succeeded, so please do not be reticent. GROUSE!

*From the Mag.*
The Recruit's Lament
By Pte. Hutt, G.M.P.

Who calls me from my nice warm bed,
Pulls off the blankets o'er me spread,
And kicks the bolster from my head?
**The Corporal**

When after months of drilling hard
My thoughts a weekend leave regard,
Who tells me I'm for Sunday Guard?
**The Sergeant**

And then with righteous wrath I swell
And say "These guards ain't worked out well"
Who tells me I can go to - - - France?
**The Sergeant Major**

When in the Ord'ly Room I fret
About the slender pay I get
Who says "You're thirty bob in debt"?
**The Quartermaster-Sergeant**

Who drills me till I'm in a daze
Gives me much slang and never praise,
And seldom gives me "Stand at Aise"?
**The Subaltern**

And when I say I've lost an aunt,
And ask if special leave he'll grant,
Who tersely answers, "No, I shan't"?
**The Captain**

And when a job the Regiment's got,
And orders fly from each big pot,
Who is it really does the lot?
**The Private.**

Death. It is with sorrow that we have to notify one more death
at Singapore. Pte. A. Dance, of "A" Coy., died on August 19th.
His funeral took place on the following day at Bidadari
Cemetery.

*From the Mag.*
Tanglin
By Pte. S. G. Tutt

My efforts at descriptive matter are, perhaps, not of extreme vividness, but in this article I will attempt a general review of Tanglin and the barracks as faithfully as possible. It is situated about three miles from Singapore, a not very comfortable walk or ride when the sun is high and fierce in its intensity; but one is apt to cast off weariness and fatigue when passing through the exquisite and picturesque scenery that retains its vivid greenness through all seasons, especially along Orchard Road – a road that immediately takes the eye for its levelness, smoothness, straightness and length, lined on each side by immense bushy trees, tall palms that rear themselves erect and stand sentinel over smaller palms that spread their huge leaves like gigantic fans. At intervals through the greenery one gets a glimpse of beautiful, artistic bungalows, and in the small villages that one passes on the way to Tanglin one can see in the gloomy interior of ill-looking shops and dwellings quaint scenes of native life.

To reach the barracks at Tanglin (which is considered to be the healthiest spot on the island) one has to turn off sharp from the main road and traverse a winding narrow ribbon of red road that runs in a gradual slope up through the centre of the golf links. On the left, built on high ground, are the officers' quarters; the whole of the barracks extends over a very wide area. Plenty of space separates each bungalow, and their distinction is from A to Z. They are lengthy and very lofty, with a wide veranda running round the whole. The interior is whitewashed and delightfully cool, while the tiled roofs (some are thatched) are supported by thirty brick pillars reaching from ground to roof.

The accommodation is for two platoons in each bungalow; or about ninety men, the dining hall in the centre acting as a barrier. After dark the only light available is from a few oil lamps, making the mosquito nets appear weird and ghostlike amid the surrounding gloom. The view that can be had from various parts of the barracks is very picturesque, parts of the landscape being hilly. To the north one can see huge rubber plantations, swamps and beautiful bungalows perched on high ground, appearing like dolls' houses. To the east, in the foreground, is a large part of the barracks, the golf links, and beyond that the Botanical Gardens reaching as far as the eye can see; in the centre, showing just above the trees, one can see the summit of a splendid palace, dazzling to the eye when the sun is shining upon it, but shadowy as the darkness creeps up.

To the south is more woodland and clusters of bush, the smoke of the factories in Singapore rising above the trees. To the west of the landscape is flat and marshy, with small native farms, backed by dense rubber trees; to the right is another plantation that rises and is lost to view. On the direct horizon are low hills, with the splendid graves of Chinese dead, like brilliant dots sprinkled by the after-glow of the departing sun. Such is the vicinity of Tanglin - our home, and some 'nest!

Condolences. We deeply regret to learn from Singapore of the death on February 16 1918 of C.Q.M.S. H. Slater, and we offer our condolences and sincerest sympathy to Mrs Slater in her sad bereavement. C.Q.M.S. Slater has been in hospital for some time but his death, due to acute bronchitis, was a great shock to his many friends in both wings of the battalion.

Congratulations. We heartily congratulate our Colonel on the honour conferred on him by his appointment to the Companionship of the Most Distinguished Order of St. Michael and St. George. Lt: Col. John Ward, C.M.G., M.P., has since the beginning of the war used his great influence for the furtherance and vigorous prosecution of the task of breaking Prussian Militarism. His great speech in the House of Commons in favour of conscription did much to reconcile the labour interest to a measure so opposed to their pre-war principles. He recognised and convinced his followers that the danger to the State demanded the sinking of all class and party considerations.

In the early months of the war the Colonel raised four battalions, viz. the 18th, 19th, 25th and 26th Middlesex Regt. Of these, the 18th, 19th. and 25th are pioneer units, and each has won high praise for its bravery and efficiency on their respective battle fronts. The doings of our Battalion are too well known to need comment here, but we would add that as our CO has cheerfully shared with us our vicissitudes, we are glad to be able to share with him the pleasure of the honour has received.

Gallant Service. In connection with one of the battalions raised by Lt. Col. John Ward, MP , the following were mentioned in despatches 28th November, 1917 by Lt. General G F Milne, CR, DSO, C. in C. Salonika Force: Lt. Col H N Blakeney, DSO, Temp Capt. W L Emery, Temp Lt. E Chadwick, No. G 20580, RSM H. Graves.

NEW YEAR GREETINGS. A Happy New Year to all our

readers! May it bring to all everything that is good! The best that could come to us all would be the news of a Victorious Peace. We hope the New Year has this in store for us. The "Festive Season" has been spent under more agreeable conditions than those which were ours twelve months ago. We were then afloat and awaiting orders to go forth to face the perils of the deep. This year begins with no such dangers confronting us. How it will end, and what will happen in the meantime, none of us can tell. That there will be changes in the Battalion is expected by all, but such changes will only affect the few. To the majority of us the outlook is one of unbroken routine work. The only break in this to which we could look forward with joyous anticipation would be the break – which the Declaration of Peace alone could bring – caused by news calling us home. Until then we must "Carry On".

Looking back over the past nine months, there is much that has happened to us which enables us to look forward to our continuance here in Hong Kong with a great amount of pleasurable confidence. We have met with an abundance of kindness from the residents. By their invitations to tea and tennis, by their gifts to sport, pleasure, and entertainment, our Hong-Kong friends have shown us their unrestrained "Good Will". This has meant more to us than can be well expressed in words; and in remembering these kindnesses all doubts are removed as to the pleasure of our continued stay. A Happy New Year to you all.

Congratulations. After three years' service with conspicuous ability, our Quartermaster receives, by regulation, promotion to a Captaincy. To Captain J. A. Boulton we tender our congratulations.

## MY COMPANION.

I am out on foreign service,
Underneath a tropic sun,
And my friends are far away across the sea;
But I've always a companion
By my side, and that is one
That no mortal, save myself alone, can see.
It is just the glorious vision
Of a girl I left behind
In the land that I am proud to call my home;
And although it's only fancy,
Though it's only in my mind,
She is always there, no matter where I roam.
When I'm marching with my comrades
In the sun's relentless glare,
When I'm resting underneath a shady palm,
She is always close beside me,
She is always standing there
With her hand upon my khaki-covered arm.
As I stand and watch the sunset
Lighting up the western sky
With its crimson and its purple and its gold,
She is there again beside me,
And I seem to hear her sighs
And her sigh expresses more than words untold.
When, at night, the stars are shining,
Or the moon reflects her beams
On the softly rippled surface of the sea

There we stand, I and my vision,
In a wonderland of dreams,
Where the world holds nothing, saving her and me.
A. O. Crane.


## "TYNDAREUS" DAY


Much water has flowed under London Bridge since February 6th of last year. A great deal has been said and written about our accident, and our conduct on that occasion has been eulogised so much that we feel it is not "up to us" to say more here in respect of the incident itself.

Out of evil comes good, we know; and the incident which has caused the 25th. to be lauded has, in my own humble opinion, done this much good – it has been the means of engendering an "esprit de corps" which had not formerly existed. If this is so – and we feel that it is – then who shall say that the mining of the "Tyndareus" was a disaster?

Deeds of heroism have been done in like circumstances on countless other occasions, and we should one and all be thankful that no incident happened during the test which we underwent off Cape L'Agulhas to bring discredit on the regiment the badge of which we wear.

We now treat the incident in a jocular vein – no lives were lost, and we can afford to look upon the matter more or less as a joke now: but at the time the gentleman with the scythe was very, very near to us, and for the fact that we evaded his ruthless sweep we should all be thankful.

We one and all regret that the original battalion will not in due course return to Blighty together, but I know that I am expressing the feeling of the whole regiment when I take the liberty of making the suggestion that this day should be duly honoured, and that an annual reunion should be arranged at a suitable place in London.

To commemorate the first anniversary, the two companies marched to the Cathedral for the Thanksgiving Service, which was conducted by our Chaplain, the Rev. Cooper-Hunt, and for which special books were provided as a memento of the service. A helpful and constructive address was given by the Bishop of Victoria.

At the conclusion of the service the battalion assembled outside, and were grouped together on the various paths to listen to a speech by our Colonel. He dealt with the mining of the "Tyndareus", and repeated the main features of the episode, which, he said. had appealed to the imagination of the British Public. In addition he read the messages from their Majesties King George and Queen Mary and in conclusion bade us fear God, honour the King, and serve our country.

A very enjoyable little supper was held in the Recreation Rooms and as usual Serg't Jones and his kitchen staff, who had been very busy throughout the day, did their part well.

The concert which followed was left in the hands of those experienced organisers, Sergt. Payne and Lt. Cpl. Filbey, the song "Another little drink wouldn't do us any harm" being one of the features of the concert. Lt. Cpl. Filbey as stage manager had his hands full throughout the evening, and carried things out without a hitch. The original "Nite-Kap Concert Party" who opened the ball were good, as usual. We regret very much that the lack of space will not permit of giving the programme in detail, but all the songs and business were greatly appreciated. We must, however, find space to mention Bandsman Folley, whose pot-pourri or melodrama, "The man who wasn't" in three acts, showed considerable ability; also Gordon Payne, whole "Fivebob or the Equivalent" was original. The two very doleful comedians, Lt. Cpl Agar and Johnny Spencer, in gags and patter were at their best: and we must thank Lt. Cpls. Perry and McKenzie and Ptes. Johnny Saunderson and H. Gravell for their contributions, which ended the first half of the programme.

The second half of the concert was opened by a pianoforte solo, the "Hungarian Rhapsody No.12 of Liszt" by Cyl. Theo Sanderson. We should like to make special note of the cello solo Godard's "Berceuse" by Pte. L. Meo, and also the violin solo, "Terentia," by Lt. Cpl. J. Meo. Sergt Blaker rendered "Annie Laurie" very sweetly.

I have purposely left mention of the only lady artist who has so far been heard at Mount Austin since the 25th Middlesex came to Hong Kong until the last. I am referring of course to Miss Enid Cooper, who has a very sweet soprano voice. Her first song "Agatha Green" is from her aunt's (Miss Margaret Cooper) repertoire. This was enthusiastically encored, and for her second song she gave "When I leave this world behind" in a wry charming manner.

We will conclude by expressing the hope that next "Tyndareus" day will see us all safely back in Blighty, and that arrangements will be made for a gathering annually of the members of the battalion to keep alive the memory of the good times we have had together.

## FEBRUARY THE SIXTH.

So much has already been written and said about our accident on the Tyndareus, off Cape Town on the night of the sixth of February, that a mere member of the battalion itself is necessarily very diffident about taking up the pen to again describe the scene. Indeed one is almost tempted to wish in the words of Mark Antony, "I had come to bury Caesar, not to praise him."

Looking back over the intervening months and having read the glorified newspaper accounts, one has to avoid the danger of over-colouring the story. It is generally true that the onlooker sees most of the game and there is that touch of romance about our accident which certainly has appealed strongly to the imagination of men.

The fifth day of February had been spent most happily in Cape Town seeing the sights. Therefore when we once again set out to sea, everybody was in the best spirits possible. After tea in the evening the great majority of us were sitting and standing about on the deck watching the sun sinking, in crimson sp1endour, in the west: dreaming our dreams and blissfully unconscious of anything which did not speak to us of joy and peace, when suddenly there was a bewildering crash which made the vessel tremble violently, followed by the downfall of tons of water which had been blown up into the air by the force of the explosion which had occurred. In a moment our pleasant dreams were shattered, our light conversation rudely interrupted, and we instinctively felt that one of the pages in our life's history was about to be written. For a few moments men stared at each other in startled amazement and then looked around them like hunted animals brought to bay. seeking a way of escape. But all around them rolled the cruel sea and overhead the stars were beginning to peep forth. But, the first brief moments passed, and everyone was cool and collected and prepared to obey orders. These latter were not long delayed and in a very little time indeed everyone was standing at boat stations wearing their life belts. Almost immediately upon the explosion followed the unearthly blowing of the siren sending forth its appeal for help and sounding in the still night air like the long drawn cry of a huge animal in pain. Indeed, so poignant was the sound that talking it over afterwards many of us agreed that it caused a creepy feeling to steal over us and sent a cold shiver down our spines.

In the meanwhile S.O.S. signals were being sent out and in about a quarter of an hour after the boat struck we were considerably eased in mind to see looming into sight two good ships. How welcome they seemed to us I cannot attempt to put into cold English. They seemed to be racing toward us and might be compared to prize dogs racing across a village green. However, we could not give them our whole attention, there was too much of the element of danger about our own situation. None of us exactly knew what was the matter but we knew by the way the boat seemed to be getting lower and lower in the water, enough to make us prepare for the worst.

It was reported that a Chinese stoker was buried beneath the fall of coal caused by the shock, in one of our bunkers, and volunteers were called for to go down and dig him out. Several of the men readily offered their services and went down under the guidance of an engineer, Their exceptional bravery was not rewarded in the way they had hoped for they had only partially liberated him, when it became necessary to close the watertight doors. The man, who had then to be left to his fate, was late liberated by the engineers after the water had been got under control, none the worse for his terrible experience. Under the personal direction of the captain of the ship and his officers and encouraged and cheered by our O.C. we, as rapidly as possible, lowered boat after boat into the somewhat turbulent waters.

All this time the rescue ships had been drawing rapidly nearer, apparently indifferent to their own danger from possibly other floating mines. We all appreciated the unselfishness of such bravery and when the leading ship was near enough to hear us we broke forth into tumultuous cheering.

Although the boats of all three ships were engaged as quickly as might be in removing the troops, it was necessarily a slow process. However, the exciting and nerve-racking proceedings were considerably relieved by the singing. Everyone who had a voice at all was lustily giving vent to the well-known strains of the "Long Long Trail" and "Tipperary". Our cheery skipper, Captain Flynn, and our stalwart Colonel did much by their inspiring presence on the bridge and by their helpful and toned advice to keep the spirits of the men at concert pitch. They stuck to their posts of duty and it was only when the last man had left the ship that the Colonel, after some pressure, consented to get into one of the boats.

In spite of the seriousness of our position it would seem as if God Himself had chosen the night so that we may be rescued. The sea, whilst rough, was not too bad for safety of a small boat, the moon was full and brightly shining in the centre of a star bespangled sky, and ships were at hand to afford their valuable aid. As a battalion and as individuals we have much for which to be thankful. It was a strange and awful experience for most of us, to be climbing down ropes or rope ladders over the side of an apparently sinking ship and then to be tossing about in mid-ocean aboard an insignificant little boat. Mal-de-mer was not the least of our troubles, whilst many of us had on this 'night of nights' our first lesson in rowing. Some of the boats with experienced oarsmen in charge made the journey from ship to ship in less than an hour. But others of the craft not so well manned were in some cases several hours before they arrived at their destination. Those in the latter boats were all exhausted by their prolonged efforts, but all alike were profoundly thankful when the time came for them to mount, on precarious ladders, the side of one or other friendly ship and stand again on a safe deck.

We would not like to close this fragmentary account of our experiences without again expressing our deep admiration for the splendidly brave work of the crews of both rescue vessels and of the exceeding great kindness of all on board both ships, in their efforts to make our stay with them as happy and comfortable as they could during the time we were with them. The night of the sixth of February in the year nineteen hundred and seventeen has for ever passed into oblivion, but the memory of that night with its exciting experiences will linger with us to our dying day and help us most feelingly to sympathise with those who are daily braving the perils of the mighty deep. Gilbert S. Watts, (L/Cpl.)

## THE TYNDAREUS.

It was most unfortunate that the Middlesex men at Tanglin Barracks were in isolation when the good ship Tyndareus arrived at Singapore towards the end of July. The news of her arrival, however, very quickly spread. and men from Normanton and the outposts soon found their way down to the docks to visit old friends and have another look at the "goal posts". The Middlesex officers entertained Captain Flynn and the ship's officers to dinner at the Hotel Europe on the first of August. A most enjoyable evening was spent. On the 3rd August the ship's officers entertained the Middlesex officers to dinner on board. A most enjoyable musical programme followed an excellent dinner, and all regretted that the stay of the ship in port was too short to allow of any more merry evenings being arranged.

## LANTERN LECTURE.

On the 10th August a most interesting lantern lecture was given in the Regimental Theatre at Tanglin by Mr. Bean, a well-known resident of Singapore. Mr. Bean's subject on this occasion was "Japan" and his lecture was illustrated by exceedingly good slides from photographs, most of which Mr Bean had taken himself during two holidays he has spent in the land of the chrysanthemum.

## APRIL 1ST, ALL FOOLS DAY.

In drawing attention to this day we do not suggest that it has any special significance when related to 25th Middlesex Regiment, although every man may look back upon the days of his boyhood with more or less of glee as he remembers the ways in which he tried to "fool" others, and it may be he can remember similar pranks of more recent date; but such is not the significance which we here attach to it. We draw attention to it merely because it is the anniversary of our landing in Hong Kong. As such we may recall the sense of relief and satisfaction which was ours on this day twelve months ago. Where shall we be twelve months hence? If our duty is completed we shall have no objection to find ourselves within sight of the shores of old England. May it be so!

## THE EPIDEMIC.

Our attention has been directed recently in ways both serious and comic to the disease which has entered the Colony. Reference is made in one of the articles this month to the comic aspect of the trouble, but its seriousness is beyond questioning. We are thankful for the wise precautions which have been taken and for the freedom from its attacks which such precautions have doubtless given us. To be cautious is wise, to be scared is foolish. The rainy season is now upon us and we hope its cleansing power will help to rid us of so unwelcome a visitation.

## Disaffection
### By Sgt. E. B. Craggs.

Why this coughing, this sneezing,
All this choking and wheezing,
These sad noises that deafen the ear?
You exclaim "What's the matter?
Why such horrible clatter?"
Every face turns to you with a sneer.

In all manners of poses,
there are men who blow noses,
While others they gasp and they splutter;
Some, almost pallid with fear,
Drop from front rank to rear:
Perhaps we can dodge it! they mutter.

If the poor Hun's motley rank
When they saw our British Tank
For Hearth and for Home they did try hard
Shall these Tanks full to the brim
With purple gargle so grim
Dismay the bold soul of the Diehard?

No! Let each Comrade In Arms
Praise our kind Doctor's charms,
Though gargling may try us most sorely
It will secure us from ills
As do those Number Nine Pills

A medicine known to Macaulay!
In drill clad, respectable,
Roll up, with receptacle.
Come, join us in this healthy pastime
Duty full or employed
You will say, quite annoyed,
"If only the first were the last time!"

## HONG KONG.

We left Singapore on July 19, 1918, proceeding to Hong Kong to join up with the rest of the battalion. We arrived there on July 26th and were allowed that day for sightseeing. We left Hong Kong on the 27th. for Russia, arriving at Vladivostok August 3rd.

*The battalion at once disembarked, and led by the Czech band and our splendid sailors from the "Suffolk" and accompanied by a tremendous crowd of people, marched through the town to a saluting point opposite the Czech Headquarters, where parties of Czech, Cossack and Russian troops, Japanese, American and Russian sailors were drawn up, all of whom (except the Japanese) came to the present as we passed, while Commodore Payne took the salute for the Allied commanders, who were all present.*
*From the book "With the Die-Hards" in Siberia by Colonel John Ward.*

A brief summary of the events in Russia immediately prior to this period might seem useful to the reader at this point, without delving too deeply into the complicated politics and policies of the time. The sources for facts are the World Book Encyclopaedia and the book which was written by John Ward, C.B., C.M.G., from which will be quoted verbatim as the journey progresses across the U.S.S.R.

Russia allied itself with France and Great Britain in the early 1900s. The country had signed a defence pact with France in 1893; mutual distrust between Russia and Great Britain caused the two countries to delay signing a similar pact until 1907, when both became fearful of the growing power of Germany. This pact completed the formation of the Triple Entente, linking France, Great Britain and Russia.

In the early months of World War I, Russian armies made great gains on the Austro-Hungarian front in Galicia. but the German General Paul von Hindenburg stopped their advance at Dannenberg in 1914. The next year the Germans forced the Russians to retreat from Poland. As the war dragged on, defeat, sickness and revolutionary propaganda undermined the morale of the Russian Army.

## WORLD BOOK ENCYCLOPAEDIA
### THE FEBRUARY REVOLUTION.

By early 1917, Nicholas II and his government were no longer able to manage the affairs of state; bread riots broke out in St. Petersburg, then called Petrograd. On March 12 (February 27 by the old Russian calendar), a committee of the Duma insisted that the Czar give up his throne. Nicholas abdicated, and the Duma set up a provisional government under Prince George

Lvov. Nicholas and his family were held prisoners for many months. The Bolshevics finally executed them in July 1918.

While the Duma was setting up the provisional government, the revolutionaries organized a soviet of workers' and soldiers' representatives at Petrograd. This Soviet, and others allied with it, held the balance of political power in Russia. But it made no immediate attempt to seize control of the government. Lenin, who had left Russia after the revolution of 1905, returned in April. But not even his Bolshevic followers agreed with his slogan, "All power to the Soviets!" In June 1917, the first All-Russian Congress of Soviets decisively rejected Lenin's plans for control of the government.

## THE OCTOBER REVOLUTION.

In July 1917, demonstrations in Petrograd and military reverses at the front menaced the provisional government. The government was reorganised under Alexander F. Kerensky, who drove the Bolshevics underground and seized their newspapers. Leon Trotsky, who had recently joined the Bolshevics, was arrested. Lenin fled to Finland. But the Bolshevics continued a campaign of sabotage and violence that came to be known as the "Red Terrors".

In August, General Lavr Kornilov, commander-in chief of the army, and a czarist, made a crude attempt to seize power, but an alliance of political groups, including the Bolshevics repulsed him. The Bolshevics took most of the credit for checking the counter-revolution. The mood of the people changed under the impact of the war and revolution.

In spring and early summer, moderate parties such as the Menshevics had controlled the Soviets. After the Kornilov affair, the people swung to more radical leadership. In mid-September, the Petrograd soviet had a Bolshevic majority for the first time. Lenin quickly recognised the advantage of this majority, and from his hiding place in Finland, he sent repeated messages to the Bolshevics in Petrograd, urging them to seize power.

Late in October, he secretly returned to Petrograd to direct the uprising himself. He appointed Trotsky as his chief lieutenant. Trotsky had been released from prison in September and was elected chairman of the Petrograd soviet in October. On the night of November 7th 1917 (October 25 by the old calendar), Bolshevic troops seized the Winter Palace and arrested the members of the provisional government. The next day the second All-Russian Congress of Soviets, opened with a Bolshevic majority which accepted Lenin's Leadership.

Kerensky fled from Petrograd in a car borrowed from the American Embassy. The Bolshevic had been almost bloodless. The Bolshevic government began its programme to take over the industries in the country.

## CIVIL WAR AND INTERVENTION.

The revolution spread quickly from Petrograd to Moscow and other large cities, but opposition to the new government developed into a full-scale civil war before the Bolshevics had time to consolidate their powers. The opposition arose in part because of the objections to the Brest-Litovsk Treaty, which Frosky signed with Germany in March 1918. This treaty, which took Russia out of World War I, surrendered vast territories to Germany. By the terms of the treaty Russia gave up Poland, Finland, the Baltic States, the Ukraine and parts of the region south of the Caucasus Mountains.

Civil War began in 1918 in the Cossack regions along the Don River. By summer the conflict had spread throughout Southern Russia and Siberia. The forces opposed to the Bolshevics became known as the Whites. The Allied Powers of Czechoslovakia, France, Great Britain, Belgium and the United States supported the Whites in 1918 and 1919. The Allies claimed to be protecting Czechoslovakian troops formerly serving with the Russian Army that had been stranded in Russia by the Brest-Litovsk Treaty.

When the Russians signed the peace treaty, the Czech troops began moving eastward along the Trans-Siberian Railway on their way to ships at Vladivostok. Red troops sought to disarm them on the way and several battles developed. The Czechs finally forced their way to Vladivostok in September 1918, but not before the incident had brought on the full intervention of several Allied powers.

The Allies also intervened in the Russian civil war for a number of less obvious reasons. Many persons in Allied countries feared that military supplies sent to the Kerensky government would fall into German hands. Others resented the fact that Russia had violated its pledge, as a member of the Triple Entente, not to make a separate peace treaty. Finally many people saw a grave threat to Western civilization in the Bolshevic movement.

Allied military forces from many countries, including France, Great Britain, Japan and the United States, entered Russia from several directions. But the Red Army eventually triumphed, for many reasons. The whites did not coordinate their activities on various fronts. They also failed to take advantage of the farmers' dissatisfaction with the Bolshevics. Most important, the Red Army held a superior strategic position in central Russia. One by one, Red forces met and defeated attacks led by General Anton Denikin in the south, General Nokolai Yudenich in Estonia, and Admiral Alexander Kolchak in Siberia.

Private Bridges was finding himself carried along by the events of war which took him from England to help defend his country; he then continued his tour of duty by helping to defend the Russians from themselves, while they had now opted out of World War I, his original need for enlisting. Nevertheless, there were orders to be obeyed for the ultimate peace of the world. This war to end all wars was worth the hardships and the losses and the sacrifices – of such was the faith of the serving man and his loved ones far away at home.

There follows a series of excerpts (indicated by italics) from Colonel John Ward's book, "Die-Hards in Siberia".

*Our barracks were outside the town of Niloy-ogol; they were very dirty, with sanitary arrangements of the most primitive character, though I believe the local British authorities had spent both time and money trying to make them habitable. The officers' accommodation was no better, I and my staff having to sleep on very dirty and smelly floors. A little later however, even this would have been a treat to a weary old soldier.*

*On August 5th I attended the Allied commanders' council. There were many matters of high policy discussed, but one subject was of intense interest. General Detriks, the G.O.C. of the Czech troops, gave in reports as to the military situation on the Manchurian and Ussurie fronts. The conditions on the Manchurian front were none too good, but those on the Ussurie front could only be described as critical and unless immediate help could be given a further retirement would be forced upon the commander, who had great difficulty with his small forces in holding any position.*

*The Allied force, now reduced to about 2000 men, could not hope to hold up for long a combined Bolshevic, German and Magyar force of from 18,000 to 30,000 men.*

*Should another retirement be forced upon the Ussurie forces, it could be carried out only with great loss, both of men and materials. The next position would be behind Spasskoe, with Lake Hanka as a protection on the left flank and the forest on the right. If this could not be held, then the railway junction at Nikolsk would be endangered, with the possibility of the communications being out with other forces operating along the Trans Baikal Railway and at Irkutsk. Under these circumstances the council decided that there was nothing left but to ask for authority from the War Office to send my battalion forward at once to the Ussurie front to render what assistance possible. I naturally pointed out that my battalion was composed of B1 men, most of whom had already done their "bit" on other fronts. –*

*About 2 pm Commodore Payne, R.N., came to my quarters and showed me a paraphrased cable he had received from the War Office. The cable authorised dispatch of half my battalion to the front. I gave the necessary orders at once. That very night, August 5th, I marched through Vladivostok to entrain my detachment. It consisted of 500 fully-equipped infantry and a machine-gun section of 43 men with four heavy-type Maxims.*

*The train was composed of the usual hopeless-looking Russian cattle trucks for the men, with tiers of planks for resting and sleeping on. A dirty second-class car was provided for the Commanding Officer and his staff.*

Vladivostok. On August 5th we left for the firing line and at all of the principle places we had route marches. At most stations the Czechs had a guard of honour and a brass band, and hundreds of troops were lined up as well. We inspired the people at all stations right up to the base, then returned to Spasskoe to get re-equipped and back again to hold the line along with the gallant Czechs until the arrival of the Japanese forces.

The Japs formed their lines fourteen miles to the rear of the original line and at the given word at the front, this line withdrew, allowing the Bolshevics to come on where the Japs were concealed. At the given word of the General leading the Japanese forces the Japs, French, Czechs and British advanced in line and inflicted severe punishment to the enemy.

*We arrived at Nikolsk in the early morning. The platform was crowded with inhabitants and two Guards of honour, Czech and Cossack, with band. At Nikolsk had recently been fought an important battle between the Czechs and the Terrorists, and we were shown a series of photographs of horribly mutilated Czech soldiers who had fallen into the hands of the Bolshevic army as prisoners of war. When one is brought face to face with their work the Bolshevics are proved to be a disgusting gang of cut-throats, whose sole business in life appears to be to terrorise and rob the peasant and worker and make orderly government impossible. We received warm welcomes at many other stations. My troops retired to quarters at Spasskoe, which I had made my forward base. Next morning with my interpreter. I visited Kraevesk and had a long conversation with the commander of the front, Captain Pomerensiv. I* personally examined the line right up to the outposts, and eventually it was decided that I would send forward 203 men with four Maxims to take up a position towards what I considered to be the threatened part of our right flank.

I had drawn up my plan of attack and the first stage of the operation had been executed, when I was brought to a standstill by a piece of fussy interference. I was to stand purely on the defensive, and not move an inch beyond my position.

I made the best dispositions possible in view of my cautious instructions, and soon every man, British, Czech and Cossack, was imbued with a determination to baulk the enemy's eastward ambitions at all costs. The numbers I had brought to their assistance were nothing compared to the influence of the sight of the poor, frayed and dirty Union Jack that floated from my headquarters, and the mosquito fires in the bivouac at night. These two factors together changed the whole atmosphere surrounding the valiant, ill-fed and ill-equipped Czech soldiers.

The day following I had fixed for the destruction of the enemy outpost, two companies of enemy infantry and three guns marched out of Schamovka as a reinforcement. At 11 pm the flash of guns was observed to our right. At 12.30 the field telephone informed me that the Czechs and the Cossacks had been shelled out of their positions, and were retreating along the roads. Disregarding the imperative instructions not to move, I advanced my detachment by a midnight march to protect the bridges and cover the retreat of our friends.

The Czechs and the Cossacks retired safely and took up new positions, while I retired to a bivouac of branches and marsh grass behind "Look-Out Hill", where for a fortnight we carried on constant warfare against infected waters and millions of mosquitoes, without transport, tents. nets, or any of the ordinary equipment required by such an expedition.

*Before leaving Hong Kong I had suggested we might find tents useful, but the proposal was turned down, either because there were none or they were considered quite unnecessary. I asked too whether I should require mosquito nets, and well remember the scorn with which the Chief of Staff greeted my question. "Who ever heard of mosquitos in Siberia?"*

*Well the fact is that while there are a few in the tropics there are swarms of these pests all over Siberia. In the tropics their size prevents them from doing much damage, except as malaria carriers. In Siberia they take the shape of big, ugly, winged spiders which will suck your blood through a thick blanket as easily as if you had nothing on. They have a knack of fixing themselves in one's hair below the cap and raising swollen ridges around one's head until it is painful to wear headgear. In my case my wrists were puffed up out level with my hands. After sleeping, one woke unable to open one's eyes. The absence of any protection wore out the patience and nerves of the men, and the searching Bolshevic shells were accepted as a welcome pastime.*

*During the fortnight of fighting off the mosquitoes, the battalion also spent days and nights counter-firing at the enemy. At one time the enemy had made direct hits on their meagre artillery, necessitating a request from the Navy to send more guns. They responded in an incredibly short space of time by sending an armoured train with two 12-pounder naval guns and two machine guns. This put new heart into the men, though they never showed the slightest sign of depression in spite of their many discomforts; the British soldier certainly offers the most stolid indifference to the most unfavourable situations.*

*General Deteriks visited the front with information of a French detachment to be joining the British troops on August 18. After the many days of fighting , the French Major Pichon and Colonel John*

*Ward reluctantly decided that a retirement was the only alternative to being completely surrounded.*

*Necessary orders were drawn up to secure the retreat. The Czechs retired first to entrain at Kraevesk, followed by the English, and the French brought up the rear as it was covered by the English armoured train, assisted by the machine-gun section of the Middlesex Regiment under Lieutenant King. So the evacuation of their splendid position regretfully began.*

### Japan Intervenes.

*The retirement was carried out as arranged in perfect order, with the loss of very little material and not more than a dozen men taken prisoner. The French were the last to entrain. The whole movement was covered by the two armoured trains under the command of Captain Bath, R.M.L.I. Before retiring, the bluejackets blew up the bridge on our front and otherwise destroyed the line in a very workmanlike manner. If we had been supported, the retirement would have been quite unnecessary.*

*The new line was held on the left of the railway by one company of Czech infantry; two British armoured trains occupied the railway, and a Middlesex machine-gun battery of four Maxims occupied the right, while the slope leading to Dukoveskoie was held by the French. The right of the village was very sparsely held by a reduced battalion of the 5th Czech Regiment and Kalmakoff's Cossacks. The whole force was under the command of Major Pichon. The enemy quickly repaired the bridges and the line, and within forty-eight hours his armoured trains were observed moving cautiously into Kravesk, our old headquarters. Simultaneously his patrols advanced from Antonovka and came into touch with Kalmakoff's scouts on the right, and three days from our retirement his advanced elements were testing our line from end to end.*

On the evening of August 22nd orders were received to push forward the observation post of our armoured trains to a spot indicated, which proved to be six hundred yards ahead of our positions and near enough to be easily raided from the enemy lines. Lieutenant T. E. King, machine-gun officer, was at the same time ordered to move forward two Maxims, with a reduced company of Czech infantry in support to protect this advanced post. The night was enlivened by constant skirmishes between British and Terrorist patrols until about 8.30 am, when it was observed that the Japanese patrols on the right had quietly retired without giving any notice of their intention, and that the enemy were in position on the plain for an attack and had already advanced along a ridge to within a hundred yards of the outpost.

The movements of the enemy were observable only from the main lookout, from which orders were already on the way gradually to withdraw the party to a position nearer the lines.

Before the order could be delivered the enemy attacked. Lieutenant King proceeded to withdraw the guns alternately, working the foremost gun himself, but defective ammunition frustrated his efforts. He gallantly tried to restart the gun, but the enemy were now upon him and he had no alternative but to retire without the gun.

The small Naval party in the advanced lookout were practically surrounded, but under Petty Officer Moffat, who was in charge, they managed to get out, with the enemy on their heels. This party was saved by a marine named Mitchell, who, seeing Petty Officer Moffat in difficulties, turned on his knee and faced his pursuers. Their fire was erratic, but his was cool and accurate, and after three of four rounds the Magyars kept their heads well down in the long marsh grass, which permitted the party to escape.

The result of this skirmish, however, allowed the enemy armoured *train to advance to a point dangerously near our defensive works, which with a little more enterprise and determination, he might easily have enfiladed. But though the enemy train had mounted a six-inch gun our twelve-pounder Navals were too smartly handled to allow any liberties to be taken.*

*This was the situation on the morning that the Japanese 12th Division began to deploy behind the new Allied line at Dukoveskoie.*

*"The Allied troops will attack the enemy, inflicting on them an annihilating disaster, tomorrow, August 24th 2h." - Part of a communiqué from Japanese command, Svagena.*

*The Battle of Dukoveskoie and Kraevesk.*

*Our road for about two miles lay alongside the railway, after which the sodden nature of the ground and the danger of losing direction in the darkness forced the men of the 25th to take to the railway. About a mile and a half along the track brought us to our armoured trains, where we were to pick up our machine-gun section, which was to act with us if necessary, or remain as a reserve or rallying point in case of need. Except for the sentries, the train crews were asleep, and were aroused and given the instructions to move forward in support of the troops in case of need and to watch the proceedings generally, to render aid to any Allied detachment which might be in difficulties. This duty was performed by Captain Bath to the satisfaction of the commanders of the French and Czech detachments.*

*The men of the 25th moved forward in file on each side of the railway track to the point selected for their rendezvous. The enemy must have anticipated the rendezvous, for the place was ploughed with shells* from end to end. The first pitched under the centre of a peasant's cottage, and in a moment cottage and peasant were no more. Five enemy armoured trains were on the line disputing every inch of our way but their schrapnel was either too high or exploded too far behind the front line that, though it made havoc amongst the laggards, it had but little effect upon those who kept well to the front.

The men of the 25th were the only "B-Oners," and the pace was beginning to tell; still they were leading, owing to the fact that their advance was alongside the railway and the usual tracks at the side. A rally was ordered by Colonel Ward and they then advanced with only such troops as could be reasonably expected to keep the line. This party numbered about sixty. They advanced within fifty yards of part of a burning train, amid a shower of debris from the exploding shells stored in its magazine. The second train looked quite deserted, and therefore beyond examining, the ammunition cart of a 5-in gun left derelict on the road; and counting ten rounds of unfired ammunition, they passed without molestation up the railway embankment on the way to Kravesk.

They had passed the trains and left them about two hundred yards in their rear when they were startled by rapid rifle shots behind them. On looking round, they were astonished to see spiteful jets of rifle fire issuing from both sides of the uninjured train, directed against thick bunches of Japanese troops who were passing along the track over which the 25th had just advanced. A Japanese officer gave the order to charge, and every man instantly bounded forward, stabbing, clubbing and bayoneting every Bolshevic they could get at. No Bolshevic was left alive to tell the reason why they allowed about sixty English officers and soldiers to pass unmolested at point-blank range of about forty yards, and only began to fire when the Japanese soldiers came under their rifles.

The progress of the 25th became very rapid after that, and except *for a few bursts of schrapnel which continued to fly harmlessly over their heads they approached their old station, Kravesk. The stuffing was completely knocked out of the Bolshevic army and the advance took more the form of beaters driving big game. The sun was very hot - the time was about 8.30 am, and this small minor action proved to be one of the most decisive of the war, as it destroyed the whole Terrorist army east of the Urals.*

*Upon orders to remain in reserve the men returned to Svagena with the proverbial luck of their battalion. The Japs had over six hundred casualties, but not one of the 25th was hit. They had many cases of prostration, but in view of the category of the unit, not more than was to be expected considering the strenuous month's work they had undertaken. One and all behaved like Englishmen, the highest eulogy that can be passed upon the conduct of men. General Oie of the Japanese unit sent a letter of special thanks to the commanding officer of the British unit for their great services in the engagement.*

*This completed the Ussurie operations, for the battle was absolutely decisive. The enemy were entirely demoralised, and never made another stand east of Lake Baikal.*

## SPASSKOE.

After that we withdrew with the French and proceeded back to Spasskoe for a well-earned rest.

*So far as the men's comfort was concerned, new roads were constructed and old ones repaired, broken windows and dilapidated walls and woodwork were either replaced or renovated. Electrical appliances were discovered and fixed, and what had previously Been a dull, dark block of brickwork suddenly blossomed into a brilliantly-lighted building and became at night a landmark for miles around.*

*We also began painfully to piece together the broken structure of society. For over a year no law but force had been known in these regions, and many old wrongdoings and private wounds demanded liquidation. We made many journeys to outlandish villages and settlements, fixed a table in the centre of the street and with the aid of the parish priest and the president of the local council, heard and decided disputes, public and private. The intimate relationship of Russian family life, from the highest to the lowest, was constantly laid bare before me with all its romance and mediaeval trappings.*

We left Spasskoe on 29-9-1918 in three trains and started on a three thousand-mile journey to Omsk, the capital of Siberia. The first place of note to reach was Nikolsk, then Harbin, where we had a route march and a short stay. On October 2nd we were given gifts in the form of soap and chocolates.

*The Allied forces in the Trans Baikal had now accomplished their task of dispersing the forces of lawlessness, and had made some progress in the work of administration, but if this work was to be consolidated and made of permanent value it must be given a centre, other than Allied command. The Allies had taken control of the far eastern provinces, but, if their object was to be carried through and German designs frustrated, it was necessary to push at once their control to the Urals and, if possible, beyond.*

*Who would think of taking a military force over six thousand miles from its base through a partially hostile country? All eyes turned to the old "Die-Hard" Battalion which had now proved its mettle on land and sea.*

*The first part of the journey was through hundreds of miles of* uncarted corn. As far as the eye could see, to left or right, was one vast sea of derelict corn, left uncared for on the land to rot in the Siberian winter. The entire absence of labour, and the complete breakdown of internal administration and communication, had produced stark want in the presence of plenty. It made one feel quite sad to look day after day upon this waste of human food and remember the food rations and regulations at home. All along the line there was a continuous stream of refugees of all nations and races - poor hunted creatures who had horrible stories to tell of the ravages of the Bulgar and the atrocities of the Bolsheviki. At one place the Serbian women and children got the breakfast of my men, the Tommies refusing to eat until the kiddies had been satisfied. And the pathetic homage they paid to our flag when they discovered it was the flag of England! I shall never forget some of the scenes which showed us also the wonderful trust the struggling nationalities of the world have in the power, humanity and honour of our country. It is a priceless possession for the world which Englishmen must forever guard.

Through apparently never ending uplands we entered the great range between Siberia and China. On and on through mountain gorge and fertile valley, we broke at last out on the wide open plains of Manchuria. The railway was under a sort of joint control, Russian, American and Japanese, and it soon became clear that one or the other of these groups was unfriendly to our western advance. The first incident was a stop of four hours, and when more vigorous enquiries were made as to the cause of delay, we were quite naively informed that the station master did not think we ought to risk going further. We soon informed him to the contrary and again started forward.

The next stop of this character was at a fairly large station about twenty hours from Harbin. I gave orders for my guard to form up across *the line at each end of the station and either bayonet or shoot anyone who tried to take the engines away. I then forced the operator to tell me if the line ahead was clear, and threatened to take the station master under arrest unless he announced my intention to start in that direction and cleared the way ahead. I put a soldier with fixed bayonet on the footplate to see that the driver held to his post and did not play tricks with the train, and started on our journey. From then on I took no risks.*

*Harbin is a conglomeration of houses of a more or less Chinese character. Elaborate preparations had been made by an Allied committee for our reception, and when we drew into the station it was crowded with a cosmopolitan crowd of Far Eastern races. Speeches were delivered, and a reply given which elicited from the Cossack band the most astounding rendition of the British National Anthem that was ever heard around the seven seas… Tea was served in a specially decorated marquee on the platform, all the men were given presents of one sort or another, and the town gave itself over to a tumultuous enjoyment, happy in the thought that at last one of Allies had appeared on the scene.*

We left Harbin October 4th at 10 o'clock. Our next stop was at Manchulli on October 6th about midnight, where we had a train losing several carriages, the cookhouse, Y.M.C.A. and Colonel John Ward's car. Fortunately number two train was just behind and pulled them to the next station, where a sorting out was again made.

We left Manchuria on October 7th, but before we left, owing to the refusal of the railway officials to meet John Ward's demands for a coach, he later "fell in" the regiment and enforced it, thus delaying us for some considerable time.

After leaving this station, number two was run into by an engine driven by a drunken Russian who was handed over to the Czechs. The collision caused the rear of the train to catch fire, but the shock was soon over and once more we proceeded on our way.

*After leaving Harbin we crossed the finest bridge of the whole journey to Omsk. It carries the railway over the River Sungary, which meanders about over the enormous, yet fairly well-cultivated, plains of Manchuria.*

*After climbing the Hingan Range the plains came as a wonder to me. Imagine if you can a perfectly flat land through which your train glides hour after hour, day after day. The whole is covered with rough grass and a growth somewhat like a horse daisy or marguerite. At the time we passed these plants had dried, and a terrific wind sweeping over the plains had broken countless numbers of the dry herb off near the ground. They fell on their rounded sides. Directly the plants had lost their anchorage, away they bounded like catherine wheels over the plains.*

*There are occasional obstructions in the shape of a huge flock of sheep which would cover half of Rutlandshire. These are herded by quaintly dressed Mongolian Tartars, on wonderful shaggy-haired horses, who ride at a furious pace around their flocks and guard them from attack by* the wolves which infest this part of the world. *Having fed off the grass and herbs in one place, the whole Tartar tribe moves forward at regular periods at what appears to be an endless crawl across the world, but what is really an appointed round, settled and definite within the territorial lands of the race to which it belongs.*

*Their women and children journey with them and hunt and ride with the men. free as the plains over which they travel. In spite of this community of interests the men seem to place very little value upon their women except as a sort of communist coolie attachment for carrying the camp from one place to another, for preparing the rude meals, and for the care of the boys, of whom the tribe is very proud.*

Over this featureless wilderness we travelled day after day, each stopping place marked by a few aspen trees mixed up with a few others that looked like mountain ash but were not. The winter houses of the people are single-roomed square, wooden structures, very strangely built, with flat roofs, consisting of about two feet of earth. Against and over these structures in winter the frozen snow piles itself until they have the appearance of mere mounds, impossible to locate except for the smoke which escapes from a few long crevices left open under the eaves of what is intended to be the front of the house. The smoke escapes perform double duty of chimneys and to keep clear the way by which the inhabitants go in and out. Their herds are either disposed before the winter begins or are housed in grass-covered dugouts, which in winter, when the snow is piled over them, take the form of immense underground caverns, and are quite warm and habitable for man and beast.

Near the end of this plain we began to encounter a few sand dunes with outcrops. Over these we gently ran day after day until we could see vast fields of sand and scrub that must have taken thousands of years of gale and hurricane to deposit in the quaint pyramidal fashion in which they stand today.

We arrived at Hazelar on a Saturday evening, and collected our echelons during the night. On Sunday morning I made application to the priest for permission to hold our parade service in the grounds of the Greek church. This was granted, and the parade was a huge success. The spectacle of the padre (Captain Roberts) in his surplice conducting the English service under the shadow of the church our help had rescued from the violence of the Terrorists was very impressive. The service was watched with intense interest by hundreds of men and women and by the crowds of Chinese, Korean and Tartar plainsmen. Some of the Russian ladies joined in the responses, and many women's voices in the old English hymns. These were the first religious services that had been held for a year, and seemed to give assurance to the people that their troub1es were nearly over, that peace had come again. The huge padlock and chain upon the church door had been removed, and general thankfulness seemed to be the predominant feeling.

A mere military parade would have failed; but with a thorough understanding of our object in entering so far into their country we gained their confidence and enlisted their help. There was not much interest in the remainder of the Mongolian and Manchurian part of the journey until we arrived at Manchulli. This was occupied by the Japanese division under the command of General Fugi. Here it was necessary to get a supply of fresh broad and exercise the horses. I paid my respects to the Chinese general, who had just lost part of his barracks, forcibly taken from him for the occupation of Japanese troops. I also paid an official visit to General Fugi and staff and the Russian commandant of the station.

It was at Manchulli that an incident happened which was much talked about at the time and was given many strange versions. It was impossible to secure proper travelling accommodation for the officers, either at Spasskoe or Nikolsk, but such would be provided at Harbin. In company with the British Consul (Mr. Sly) I called upon the manager of the railway at Harbin to secure such accommodation, but no carriage was available. He could do nothing, but said there were plenty at Manchulli, held up by Colonel Semianoff and the Japanese, who took hold of every carriage that tried to get through the station. l was prepared to take the risk and use force if necessary. I should be able to get them there.

The weather was getting very cold, with each mile adding to their discomfort. The only accommodation for officers and men was in cattle trucks. Can one begin to imagine the discomforts of sitting hour after hour, and day after day on the wooden planks used at night for beds to sleep upon? Colonel Ward was in hopes of being able to secure at least two more carriages from the Japanese division, but after asking through the official channels and waiting for two hours for the carriages to be shunted on to one of his three trains, it was obvious that the "Power" at the station had no intention of giving up the carriages.

It was there and then I made up my mind to act, and if necessary to go the "whole hog". I informed the authorities that nothing should be shunted in that station until those two carriages were joined to my trains, and proceeded to occupy the whole station. Up to this point I had neither seen nor heard anything of the Japanese in relation to this matter, but they now came on the scene, and I soon discovered that it was they who had engineered the whole opposition to the British officers getting suitable accommodation. At first they did not know the correct line to adopt, but made a request that the guard should be taken off the station. Colonel Ward said yes instantly, if it is understood that these carriages are to be shunted by my trains. They agreed to this and my guards were taken off, having held the station for twenty-three minutes. I had my evening meal, and was expecting to start when I was informed that the Japanese had now placed guards upon my carriages and refused to allow them to be shunted on to my train. I thought this was just about the limit and before taking action decided I had better discover the reason, if any, for what seemed a definite breach of faith.

I visited the Japanese station officer and he said they had just discovered that these two carriages were set aside to convey General Fugi to Harbin a few days hence. I refused to believe that such a discovery could have only just been made, and said I would take the carriages by force if necessary. It looked very awkward , I sent my liaison officer (Colonel Frank) to find the station commandant who had allocated the cars to me. The Japanese staff officer was expressing his apologies for my not being able to get any carriages for my officers when in stalked the old Russian commandant and blew these apologies sky high by declaring that these carriages had nothing to do with General Fugi's train, that they were unemployed and that they were mine. I decided to strengthen the guard to eighteen men on each carriage, and offered protection to the railwaymen who shunted them onto my train. The Japanese soldiers followed the carriages onto my train, so that we had the strange sight of a row of Tommies with fixed bayonets on the cars and a row of Japanese soldiers on the ground guarding the same carriages. No officer came to give them open orders, but the Jap soldiers disappeared one at a time until the Tommies were left in undisputed possession.

I do not suppose there was any real danger of a collision between the different forces at Manchulli, but it had the appearance of a very ugly episode that might have developed into one of international importance.

We arrived at Chita without further incident of importance. Bread and horse exercise delayed us one whole day, and inability to secure engines part of another, until in desperation I went with a squad of men to the sheds and forced an engine driver to take out his engine, I myself riding on the tender, where I nearly lost my sight with hot debris from the funnel, while Major Browne, who stood sentinel beside the driver, had holes scorched in his uniform.

The next point of interest was Lake Baikal, or as it is more correctly described by the Russians, the Baikal Sea. We approached this famous lake on a very cold Sunday evening, and long before we reached its shores the clear cold depths of the water gave evidence of its presence in the changed atmosphere. A furious gale was blowing which lashed huge waves on the rock-bound shore, blinding snow mixed with the spray giving the inky blackness of the night a weird and sombre appearance.

*We put up the double windows, listed the doors and turned in for the night. We all awoke early to find the scene so changed as to appear almost miraculous. The strange light of the northern zones was gently stealing over an immense sea of clear, glassy water. A fleecy line of cloud hung lazily over the snow-capped mountains. The stars shone with icy cold brilliance and refused to vanish, though the sun had begun to rise. And such a rising. A beautiful orange and purple halo embraced half the world, from its centre shot upwards huge, long yellow streamers which penetrated the darkness surrounding the stars. Gradually these streamers took a more slanting angle until they touched the highest peaks and drove the cloud lower and lower down the side of the mountains. There is nothing in the world like an autumn sunrise on Lake Baikal.*

*Rumour says there are exactly the same kind of fish in Lake Baikal as in the sea, with freshwater fish added to them, Seagulls of every known category are found there, and wild duck in variety and numbers also. Passing along this wonderful panorama for some hours, we arrived at Baikal. The lake is fed by the River Selengha, which drains the northern mountains and plains of Mongolia. It is drained to the west by the famous River Anghara, which rises near Baikal, and enters the Polar Sea at a spot so far north as to be uninhabitable, except for the white bears who fight for possession of the icebergs.*

We arrived at Chita on the 10th and on the 11th passed Lake Baikal – 500 miles long – arriving at Irkutsk on the 14th and departing on the 15th. We passed on to Zema, where the Bolshevics were causing great trouble. As soon as our trains arrived in this station the drivers were forced to leave their posts, leaving us without drivers.

*Irkutsk, situated on the right bank of Anghara, is a rather fine old town for Siberia. Its Greek Cathedral has a commanding position, and* contests successfully with the Cadet School for supremacy as the architectural feature first to catch the eye. The town is approached by a quaint, low wooden bridge which spans the swiftly-running river. When we saw it the battered remnants of human society were grimly collecting themselves together after some months of Bolshevic anarchy and murder. Whole streets were mere blackened ruins, and trade, which had been at a complete standstill, was just beginning to show a return to life.

The 25th Battalion, Middlesex Regiment, was the only British unit in the country; it had spread itself out in a remarkable manner, and shown the flag on a front of 5000 miles. In spite of its category it had brought confidence and hope to a helpless people out of all proportion to its strength and ability. A public banquet (the first since the Revolution) was held, ostensibly to welcome Volagodsky, the Social Revolutionary President of the Siberian Council, but really to welcome the first British regiment that had ever entered and fought in Siberia. It was a great occasion, and the first real evidence of possible national regeneration.

The day following we marched to the square space surrounding the Cathedral. It was altogether a fine and impressive sight, with big crowds and, with the "President" and "The King" at the end, every man present uncovered, an old Russian lady knelt and kissed my adjutant's hand and blessed us as saviours, "saviours", while the commandant asked for cheers for "the only country which came to our help without conditions".

The sentiments of the people changed completely every few hundred miles. After leaving Irkutsk we soon discovered that we were in enemy territory, and the few weeks, in some cases days, that had elapsed since the retirement of the Bolshevic Commissars had left the country the prey of the desperado.

That night we ran into Zema station, where we came to a sudden stop. I sent my liaison officer to find the cause, and he informed me that a body of men were beside the engine and threatening to shoot the driver if he moved another foot.

I ordered the "Alarm" to be sounded, and instantly 400 British soldiers tumbled out of the trucks. Taking their pre-arranged positions, they fixed bayonets and awaited orders. My carriage was the last vehicle of the train. I walked forward to find the cause of our enforced stoppage, and was just in time to see a squad of armed men leaving the station. I took possession of the station and telegraphs, and then heard from the officials that Bolshevic agents had come to the town and had persuaded the workmen to leave work, to take arms and cut the line to prevent the Allies moving forward, and await the arrival of the Bolshevic forces. This force had worked its way along the Mongolian frontier towards the line to destroy the railway over the river Ocka. Our guards were placed around the engine sheds and railway works and approaches, and occupied by force the post office and telegraph office in town. Orders were given that all men must pledge themselves not to interfere with the trains, and return to work by 6 a.m., or they would be dealt with by martial law.

Two hours elapsed, by which time our other trains arrived, with machine-gun section complete, and the whole force were disposed to receive attack. Colonel Ward interviewed the spokesman for the workers and eventually most of them reported back to work. Those who did not were given the opportunity to air their grievances, which led Colonel Ward to conclude that it was more of a military movement on the part of the Bolshevics than a workers' strike. The business of the Battalion was to leave Zema as soon as possible, but to leave the line safe for further Allied travellers. Hence he ordered surrender of all arms by the inhabitants, and allowed 12 hours in which this was to be done.

That evening the time limit expired. The inhabitants of Zema suddenly found machine guns in position ready to spray all their main *thoroughfares with lead should the occasion arise. Sections of the town were searched house by house, until the piles of arms necessitated transport to remove them. In some houses dumps of looted fabrics taken from other towns were taken into possession.*

*The Echo of Zema travelled far and wide, and gave the authorities an object lesson how to tackle the cancer as deadly as it was devilish.*

## KRASNOYARSK.

Every available man fell in with plenty of ammunition and spread us in directions; and on the following day we made a house to house search for arms etc., and several guns and rifles were taken, all in all about four cart loads.

That trouble over, we carried on to Krasnoyarsk, where we arrived on the 20th. After a route march we left "C" Company to garrison the town with the assistance of an Italian regiment. We left on the 24th October and arrived at Omsk on the 26th and a guard of honour was waiting for us, and after various speeches we had a decent bust up to celebrate our arrival at the capital of Siberia. After living in the trucks for a short period we went to barracks November 2nd. We first heard of Germany's downfall on November 12th. Several alarms were given before Christmas, but up till that time no serious trouble occurred.

*When the old Russian Army was destroyed, sixteen million soldiers took their rifles and ammunition home. This was the insoluble problem of every attempt to re-establish order in the Russians' dominions. The Middlesex made their first plunge at Zema, and others soon followed along the path. They re-armed the local militia and took the rest of the confiscated arms to Omsk, where they were taken over by the Russian authorities for the new Russian army.*

*At midnight the 25th. started on their further journey. They had been passing through hundreds of miles of wonderful virgin forests for the last two weeks, with an occasional opening for village cultivation and an occasional log town. Approaching Krasnoyarsk, the hills and valleys were covered with pine trees and frozen rivers, looking like a huge never-ending Christmas card.*

*At last they arrived at Krasnoyarsk, a large struggling town of great importance on the River Yenisei. As they approached they passed miles of derelict war material - tractors, wagons, guns of every kind and calibre all cast aside as useless, there being no place where defects could be repaired. Some had no apparent defects, but there they lay, useful and useless, a monument to the entire absence of organisation in everything Russian.*

*We remained in Krasnoyarsk for two days, finding the town in a disturbed condition, as it was necessary to guard the great bridge there. A quarter of the company remained under the command of Captain Eastman, O.B.E., in the excellent barracks which had been prepared for the unit. This place had originally been fixed upon as the station for the whole of the battalion, but important events were happening in Omsk; the train started off during the night, and on the evening of the next day we arrived at Hachinsk, where we were greeted by a Russian guard and a priest who presented us with bread and salt, as befits a Tartar who welcomes a friend.*

*At last we arrived in Omsk, the end of our journey, having passed a zigzag direction almost around the world. A few miles to the Urals and Europe again. So near and yet so far.*

*October 18th, and a right royal welcome awaited us. The station was decorated with flags of all nations, the Russian for the first time dominating. We were introduced to all and sundry and began to mix wonderfully well. Their welcome was doubtless tinged with relief at the security afforded by the presence of well-disciplined troops. I had a few moments for conversation with Sir Charles Eliot, our High Commissioner, on the political situation. I gathered that a desperate effort was being made to join the Directorate of Five, which stood as the all-Russian government and received its authority from the constituent Assembly at Ufa. The English and the French representatives were genuinely anxious that a cabinet be formed that would give confidence to moderate Russian opinion, and so command Allied recognition.*

*But advice is one thing, accomplishment another. It was impossible to expect that hundreds of years of tyranny and bad government could be swept away by the waving of a diplomatic wand.*

*To combine the hostile and divergent elements of the Siberian government, Revolutionary and Royalist, Cossack, Socialist and "Intelligentsia" with the Ufa Directorate seemed impossible. But the "Politicals" thought otherwise. They were guided by the highest motives and they gave their very best in the interest of the Russian people, but they tried to accomplish the unattainable. The most that could be said of their policy is that it was worth attempting. Try they did, and under the influence of the Bolshevic guns booming along the Urals and a Royalist conspiracy at Chita a piece of paper was produced with a number of names upon it bearing the resemblance of a workable arrangement between opposites.*

*One thing, however, had been done which was fated to have important after-effects. Vice-Admiral Koltchak had been brought into the new Council of Ministers with the title of Minister for War. On November 6th 1918 we were all invited to a banquet in honour of this new all-Russian government. It was to be the climax of all our efforts and a tangible evidence of the successful accomplishment of a great diplomatic task.*

*The business at Omsk went on much as usual, but Omsk society became more subdued in its whisperings. The Allies were pushing forward supplies for the new armies facing the Terrorists along the Ural front, but it was soon discovered that such arms were being deflected from their proper destination.*

As regards Christmas at Omsk, it is not worth mentioning as it was such a miserable turnout, that readers would be disgusted to learn the truth. After Christmas we had a medical board and besides the 135 unfit men a large number were graded unfit for Siberia; I was attached to "A" company on 8th of January as only "A" company are remaining at Omsk and several of "B" and "D" company are temporarily attached to make them up to strength.

The Hampshire 1st Company arrived on the 6th and the 2nd company arrived on the 7th January and was transported to barracks by our regimental transport. The remaining two companies arrived on Friday 8th.

On Saturday we had a concert, and on Sunday we received the Christmas puddings from England, which came in very useful while on guard. We received gifts of socks and gloves from the Canadian Red Cross. Also received ten packets of cigarettes and some chocolates.

On Monday "D" Company and "B.2" and "B.3" packed their kit ready for Vladivostok and Krasnoyarsk. Tuesday January 14th guard in honour of officers receiving decorations, amongst them Col. John Ward, M.P., C.M.C., who received the French Croix de Guerre. Ten men at least got frostbitten, as it was severely cold.

During December I was on a course of machine-gunning and after the class had been formed a fortnight, a fatal accident occurred, and I was an eye witness and attended the inquest which was as expected "Accidental Death"!

"D" Company and details left Wednesday January 15th. Death of Private Fuller, "A" Company, transport driver, making the fourth at Omsk.

Saturday 18th photographs taken in furs at 30 roubles per half dozen. Sunday 19th, anniversary of departure from Singapore actually 6 months, received gifts of tobacco and woodbines. Funeral of Private Fuller 20th January. I was picked for the firing party. Owing to the intense cold we did not fire any volleys but did all the ceremonial motions. Saturday January 25th, inspection by Canadian doctor.

Death of Bert Martin in Manchuria en route to Vladivostok. He was L/C. of "B" company. Thursday January 30th, received one pair of mittens. Medical inspection February 1st. 1919. Thursday Feb. 6th., second anniversary of the Tyndareus (report at end of book). Monday Feb 10th, a Cossack was caught in the stables trying to thieve a horse, and was arrested and handed over to his regiment. (fate not known).

REPORT FOUND AT END OF DIARY.
Second Anniversary of Tyndareus Accident
1919 February 6th.

Menu For the Day.
Breakfast. Porridge, Steak and Onions,
Bread and Butter and Tea.
Dinner. Roast Pork, Beans, Mashed potatoes, Duff with Jam
Tea. Buns, Butter, Jam, Cakes, Biscuits, Tea.
Rum Ration. Double Issue 6 o'clock.
Supper. Bully Beef Sandwiches, Custard.

Band selections played in the room. At the conclusion of the 10.30 service Colonel J. Ward gave a speech explaining how we were saved, as the hole in the ship being large enough (27ft. by 11ft) to allow the cargo of machinery to drop into the Indian ocean and by the luck that No 1 hold pump was in the left side of the ship.

Friday February 14th: a severe wind and snow storm and guards had to withdraw. Buildings and sheds blown everywhere.

Duty 9-10.

Warned to proceed on duty as butcher with Col. Ward. Issue of Canadian kit on 14th. Drew Arctic pay Wednesday 19th. Entrained for Krasnoyarsk, arrived Tuesday 25th

Col. John Ward's tour to Krasnoyarsk.

Party consisted of sixteen men, two serg'ts, R.A.M.C. (Burgess, Corporal) Cook (Butcher & Quartermaster). Officers- Col. John Ward; Col. Franks; Jock Golden; L/C Norman, Fred Wright (cook); Escort Cook Lewis; Acting Quartermaster and butcher etc., A. Bridges; Serg't Seager, Serg't Starsmere: Drake, Manchine: Gunners -Garrod, Spinks, Golds, Mayhew, Fennel, Brothers, Cooper, Ellingham etc. etc.

Entrained at Omsk siding Wednesday 19th. and were placed at No.1 platform A good number wanted to come inside cookhouse and I had my work cut out to eject them.

Bought box of Three Castle Cigars for 68 roubles, 75 kopaks at 2/75 per packet. We left Saturday and had a various assortment of mishaps along the route. At Bertall a carriage occupied by 18 men started falling to pieces and another one had to be commandeered. Wheels of nearly all the trunks got overheated in turn and several stops had to be made in consequence. People thought our train was a passenger train and we had a hard job keeping them out, several rows occurring, Col. Franks stepping in every time to settle the matters.

During our first night's journey the lock of the store truck was forced and taken as well as a little of the stores. The truck nearest the engine nearly collapsed, and new wheels were put on. After a sterling three days we arrived at Krasnoyarsk, Tuesday 25th. We spent the night there and after drawing a few stores we left there at two o'clock on Wednesday, and passed over a fine bridge half a mile out of town and arrived at Irkutsk on the 27th.

*While at Omsk the work of the Allied representatives was in conferences based upon the conditions of the Russian workers, and whether it was possible to do anything to help them. British officers were making desperate efforts, also, to organise a death blow to the Bolshevics in the early spring. Then there suddenly arose another sinister figure which threatened to upset all their calculations, a well-timed revolt of the railway workmen, calculated to cripple all communications, making the movement of troops and supplies impossible. They had previously been informed that Bolshevist agitators had passed through their lines on this treacherous mission, but for months nothing had been heard of the emissaries of mischief. Time was drawing close to the 1919 operations of the Perm Offensive, while rumblings of an unmistakable character were heard in all directions. This was the problem with which the Allies had to deal. with only a few weeks at their disposal. To the Russian workman it was a social question; to the Allies it was both social and military.*

Finally General Knox was to call upon Col. John Ward to undertake a pacific propaganda along the railway to see if it were possible to persuade the workmen to keep at work and give the best service possible to their country to secure the restoration of order.

At the outset he was faced with the difficulty of not being in a position to offer anything definite to the workmen in return for their willingness to assist the combatant branch of the Russian service in its crusade against anarchy. With nothing to offer, it seemed a hopeless task to ask for much. The only man who could pledge the Government was the Supreme Governor himself. So Col. Ward wrote this to him:

To His High Excellency, Admiral Koltchak, Supreme Governor.

Sir. I have been requested by Major-General Knox, Chief of British Military Mission, Siberia, to undertake a tour of the railway works along the Siberian Railway to address the workmen, and appeal to them as a British Labour representative to give their best service to the Russian State during the present and coming military operations, and to join no strike movement or to hamper the transport of men and supplies until the military operations against the enemy are completed. I have pointed out to General Knox that, while I am quite willing to undertake this mission to the railway workmen, I feel it will be quite useless unless I can promise, on behalf of the Russian government, some improvement in their condition.

1 For instance, I am informed that some of the railway and other Government workmen have not received any wages upon which to keep themselves and their families for, in some cases, many weeks, and in other cases many months. If this is true it is impossible to expect workmen to be satisfied, and the wonder would be that that they agree to work as well as they do. It would be necessary for me to be able to promise that such things would be rectified, and wages paid in the future.

*2 There are many things absent in Russia which industrial communities like England find necessary elements for industrial peace. I admit that very little constructional reform work can be executed during the present disturbed condition of the country, but it would help immensely if I could tell the workmen that I had the authority of the Russian Government that directly order had been restored, laws for the, protection and help of the Russian workmen and their organisations, on the lines of those already working effectively in England, would be adopted by the Russian Government. If I could get something definite from Your High Excellency upon these points, I believe it would do much to help in the work for the pacification of the labouring classes of Russia, and greatly strengthen Your Excellency's hold upon the hearts of the Russian people.*

*(Signed) John Ward. (Lt. Colonel, M.P. C.M.G., Commanding 25th Bn. Middlesex Regiment)*

*Omsk*

*February 15<sup>th</sup> 1919*

*Sir, In reply to your letter of February 4th, I wish to inform you that I have learned with the greatest satisfaction that you are willing to undertake the important mission of addressing the workmen of our railways and calling them to give their best service to the cause of Russia in this crucial moment of our national existence. The two questions you have raised in your letter should not be left without a prompt answer, and I would therefore like to bring to your knowledge the following:*

*1   The imperative necessity of regular and orderly payment of wages to the workers has been the object of my personal anxiety, and pressing* measures in that direction have been urged by the Government. The railways being considered just important as the army, you will understand that everything in its power will be done by our Government to help the threatening situation in that respect.

2   As for the second question which you have mentioned in your letter, I venture to assure you that the Government has already stated in its official programme that the workmen will find protection and help in the laws which shall be enforced and have to secure their organisation on lines similar to those of democratic states in Europe. The Government has a special Department of Labour which is preparing the future legislation on this question, following the general course of constructive reform work which I hope to pursue with all the energy and vigour that the military situation will permit.

I take this opportunity to renew the expression of my profound appreciation of the interest you take in our situation and of the valuable assistance that you so generously offer in this most important matter of pacification of the labouring classes in Russia.

Yours sincerely
(Signed) A Koltchak.

This is believed to be the first correspondence ever conducted by the head of any Russian Government upon a purely labour subject: It shows that in supporting Admiral Koltchak we had at least this fact to recommend our policy. Colonel Ward writes that he was a democrat, and anxious that his country should be in labour matters amongst the first flight of nations.

The Question now, What attitude would the anarchist adopt to this new evangelism?

I was ready to start on my journey when there began such a blizzard as is occasionally described in the literature of Polar exploration. For forty-eight hours from the south came a furious gale. It was not too cold, only about twenty degrees of actual frost, but with the wind came blinding snow - not snow such as we see in England, but fine snow, like white dust. It beat on your face, found its way between the flaps of your head-covers, where it thawed and ran down your neck and chest and saturated your underwear. It smashed straight on to your eye-balls, and froze in cakes to your eyelashes and cheeks, so that in five or ten minutes you were blind and unable to move in any direction. All sentries had to be withdrawn and sent to the nearest shelter, for it was impossible to locate oneself or to see a building till you blundered up against it. Roofs were torn off the houses, and the strongest buildings rocked in the most alarming manner. The snow piled itself up against the houses till it covered the windows on the ground floors and half-way up those of the second. This southern gale took twenty four hours in which to blow itself out, and four days calm followed, during which the snow was cleared from the railway and traffic resumed. The next startler was a message from Irkutsk stating that a terrific gale was breaking down from the north - a recoil from the one just described - accompanied by sixty degrees of actual frost, making it impossible to live out of doors. This storm struck Omsk on February 20th, and no words can describe the complete obliteration of man and all his works accomplished by such a gale.

Nothing can live in the intense cold created by such a wind. Hence movement and life cease, and King Frost has the whole field to himself. In a few hours the earth is levelled; all the indications made of the ordinary log dwellings are a few snow-banks with a row of dark posts from which smoke is emitted, showing that there are human habitations underneath. By February 22 this storm had worked itself out and we were able to proceed.

*On the way to Krasnoyarsk some evidence was to be seen of a recent attack by revolters, and the officer of the detachment of troops here suggested it might be well to look out for snipers and worse should the train come to a standstill. We arrived at Krasnoyarsk however without incident, on Feb. 25th, then on to Irkutsk for the 27th, and my campaign began.*

*Meetings were held at Irkutsk, and hecklers of a band of ruffians were skilfully answered by Madame Frank, the editress of the "Russian Army", as correspondent for this labour mission. The influence of this little lady upon this simple Russian workmen was really remarkable.*

We arrived at Alenta 10 o'clock Saturday morning. In the afternoon we went out shooting with Col. John Ward with little result. In the evening we went on to the station platform, where plenty of Russians were quarrelling and fighting. Left Alenta 7.30 Sunday Mar 9th, arriving at Kansk March 10th, where there was the usual wind-up. Departed Tuesday and arrived at Krasnoyarsk Wednesday March 12 at 8 o'clock at night. It was not long before trouble commenced for Col. Franks. His wife and Colonel Ward were at the station where some Serbians were drinking heavily and causing unpleasantness to other people. By request Colonel Franks went out to try and stop them. It appears he guarded the blow with one hand and drew his revolver with the other and shot the soldier dead. Colonel Franks received a deep cut on his head, and his hand nearly severed. Thursday night terrible wind-up in case of attacks, all guards doubled. We felt more relieved when we left, which was on March 20th.

*From the Regimental Mag.*
A DIE-HARD'S LAMENT AT KRASNOYARSK.

Damn Siberia's winter snows
That numb a fellow's hands and toes,
And paint his nose a purple bright,
And make him swear from morn till night.

Sometimes it's bread o'er spread with lard,
Or bully beef and biscuit hard.
There's seldom bake or a duff for you,
But often enough the Army stew

We're clothed with fur from top to toe
More like a gang of Esquimaux:
But the East wind blows through each old fur boot,
And we look in our coats like sacks of soot.
But I hope our tale of woe's near ended
All noses dried and tempers mended,
And back in 'Blighty' we soon shall be,
With plenty of yarns from across the sea.

G. C. Dance, Private.

We stopped at a small station where a company of Czechs were
and learned that the Bolshevics were in the district, and liable
to attack anywhere within the radius of 100 verts. The Czech
colonel would not hold himself responsible for our safety, but
Col. J. Ward ignored the warning. Orders were given to the

driver to go at full speed over the danger zone, and we all stood by with arms and ammunition ready for emergencies.

It was a terrible time and we never knew what was going to happen next, but providence was with us and we arrived at Zema at five o'clock. We stayed a short time there and then carried on to Irkutsk, where we arrived at 2 o'clock on Friday morning, February 28th. Four of us went to a Russian worker's home and had a good time. I was much surprised, such a clean respectable home, with a piano and violin, The family consisted of man, woman, three boys and two girls.

We left Irkutsk on March 4th and stayed a short time at Hoffercher, 30 burets from Irkutsk. We left for Zema and arrived there at two thirty Thursday, and left on Friday 7th.

*Our next stop was Imokentievskaya, where the head of the works looked as though he would have preferred execution rather than take part in a workmen's meeting. The professionals had been left behind, and the audience was composed of entirely the railway workers. They presented the characteristics of the average English workmen and hungrily received information relating to the methods of the best organised English trade unions.*

*At Zema, the scene of a sharp encounter with armed strikers a few months previous. The meeting in the works was a great success. It was remarkable that in a previous meeting with these workers we took the attitude of military dictator; they showed no resentment and had rigidly observed the agreement which had been entered into at the point of bayonet. They were delighted to find that we too had performed our part of the contract in not forgetting their interests when opportunity presented itself.*

*Nesniodinsk was not on our list, but by special request from the workmen there, we made the necessary arrangements and visited this place on Sunday March 8th.*

*Our carriage was fastened to the rear of a slow-moving train going west, and we did not arrive at Kansk till the evening of the 10th. Kansk is the most easterly point of the area of revolt and a fairly large depot for the railway. We held a splendid meeting and it was quite clear that the Russian workmen were tired of the Revolution. They merely wanted to be shown a way out of a social nightmare.*

*We started for Krasnoyarsk on the 12th, and before long found it necessary to get the machine guns and hospital equipment ready for use. After standing to arms we arrived at mid-day on the 13th, at Klukvinah, the Russian Headquarters, and discovered that the government forces had driven the enemy back from the Railway, and that the remainder of our journey to Krasnoyarsk would be practically safe. We arrived about 9.15 pm.*

*Colonel Frank, Madame Frank, I and the Czech interpreter, Vladimir, were passing through the station on our return from the town about 12.30 am, when a rather exciting thing happened. The station commandant approached Colonel Frank and appealed to him for help to send home a party of Serbian soldiers who had procured drink without payment at the points of their swords and revolvers, and had stripped a young woman passenger and exposed her for their orgies. Other bestial things were alleged against them, but no one had so far dared to interfere to restore order. After a moment's consideration Colonel Frank decided to go into the buffet and ask them to go quietly home, and if they refused. to secure force to arrest and remove them. I naturally followed.*

*It was a big stone-floored room with the door at one end and a long* bar at the other. The alleged Serbian soldiers were seated in a cluster on the right in front of the bar at the far end of the room. Colonel Frank advanced to them and said, "Brothers, you have had enough to drink, you are keeping all the attendants from their proper rest; it is time for you to go home." It was like an electric shock. About a dozen of the ruffians sprang to their feet, hurling every possible Slavonic epithet at this brave Russian officer who was merely performing a public duty. One dark-visaged cavalryman drew his sword and tried a lunge across the table, and while the Colonel watched this infuriated aborigine, a Serbian officer close behind Frank tore the epaulette from the Colonel's uniform and trampled it underfoot, shouting, "Death to this officer of the old regime!"

I picked up the epaulette just as the other Serb, sword in one hand and revolver in the other, edged round the tables to the centre of the room for his attack upon my liaison officer. I did not think of drawing my own weapon, ' , and so far it was man to man. Colonel Frank kept his eye fixed upon his antagonist and now advanced towards him, ordering him to put down his arms and leave the room. But the Serb was out for blood and made a slash at the polkovnika's head, the full force of which he evaded by ducking, though the sword severed the chin strap and button of his cap and carved its way through the thick band before it glanced up off the skull, helped by his right hand, which had been raised to turn the blow. At the same instant Colonel Frank fired point blank at man's face; the bullet entered the open mouth and came out of his cheek, which merely infuriated the man more. Up to this moment the man had only used his sword, but now he began to raise his revolver. Before he could raise it hip high, however, the Colonel shot him through the heart. Though the revolver dropped from his helpless hand, he crouched for one instant and sprang, clutching at the Colonel's *face, while four or five of his fellow Serbs attacked the Colonel from behind. The foremost of these ruffians, a Serbian officer, fired at the back of the Colonel's head and missed, but his second shot struck Colonel Frank on the left temple at the moment his real assailant had made his death spring, and down they both went, apparently dead, the Serbian on top. The other Serbians sprang forward to finish the Russian officer with the usual ugly dagger which Serbian robbers always carry. The body of the dead Serb, however formed a complete shield, and this, coupled with the fact that we all thought the Colonel dead, saved him from mutilation.*

*I was not quite an idle spectator, but the fact that at the critical moment I discovered I had no weapon except for my cane reduced me to helplessness so far as dealing with this gang of murderers was concerned. Directly the fight began, every Russian. including the armed militia man who was supposed to keep order at the station, bolted from the room, leaving the women and children to look after themselves. Madame Frank went to the assistance of her husband and covered him as only a woman can, and as she grasped her husband's revolver the Serbs slunk back a pace, while I lifted his head and signed to the Serb officer who had fired at the Colonel from behind to lift the dead Serb off the Colonel's body. This he did, and then proposed to the band surrounding us that they should kill us all three. Their knives glistened and a small automatic revolver was making a beeline for me, when a voice like the growl of a bear came from the direction of the door.*

*The whole band instantly put up their weapons. I had stood up to receive my fate, and over the heads of our would-be murderers I saw a tall dark-bearded stage villain in a long black overcoat which reached to the floor stalk across to the group. He looked at the body of the dead Serb and then at the prostrate Russian officer, who at that instant began*

*to show signs of returning consciousness. "Ah! Oh! Russky polkovnik,"
he roared, drawing his revolver. "Our dead brother demands blood."*

*I could not stand and see a wounded friend murdered before my
eyes, not even in this land of blood. I stepped both bodies and placed
myself between this monster and his victim. I raised both hands and
pushed him back, saying, "I am Anglisky polkovnik and I will not
allow you to murder the wounded Russian officer." He answered that
he was "Serbian polkovnik", and I said "Come into the other room,"
and by strategy got him away. His friends, however, told him something
which sent him back quickly to finish his job, but as he re-entered the
buffet he encountered about a dozen British and Czech soldiers with
fixed bayonets, and it was not so difficult now to convince him that it
was not quite good form to murder a wounded man.*

*We carried the Russian colonel to the British hospital, and as the
leader of the Serbs had declared a blood feud, extra guards were placed
on my wagon and the hospital.*

We stopped at a small station the following day, where John
Ward had his speech and then carried on to Tagir, which was
reached about 6 o'clock Saturday 22nd. About 8 to 8.30 whilst
stationary on the siding a shot was fired very near to us, followed
by another a short time later coming too near to us to be
pleasant. The person or persons all unknown who committed
the deed saw an escort on its way back from Omsk, among them
being Sergt. Chatzen, George Wibley and Bill Tenant. At the
station en route a crowd of men and women and children tried
to get into our truck as passengers, but as we had retired for the
night the door was corded up from the inside.

I put my head out of the window and told them who we
were and that they could not come in, but in spite of all that

they all got their weight on the door and burst it open. By this time I had my rifle and bayonet ready and at the sight of these weapons they soon withdrew again. We arrived at Noble Nichalieus (Novo Nikoliosk) Monday 24th and departed the same night, and arrived at another station the following day where another meeting was held. On Wednesday we left for Omsk, arriving back on the 26th of March.

Nothing happened on the journey to Perm, and we arrived back at Omsk Saturday May 3rd.

*We were now entering the districts behind the Ural front. These towns had not long been cleared of the Bolshevics The new Russian armies were rapidly pushing forward. We stopped for a meeting at Tumen, then on to Ekaterinburg. It was too sad to think that this was the place where the Tsar and his family were imprisoned and murdered. The meeting here proved to be one of the most remarkable gatherings. A sea of faces under huge multi-coloured "papahas" spread over the floor, while every carriage was covered with human ants; even the beams of the building carried their human freight. Clearly it seemed to me that the destruction of Russia began from the head, but its rebirth is from the ground.*

*Krasnoyarsk is a huge railway depot with building and repair shops employing about 3,000 workmen. To get at both shifts it was necessary to hold two meetings. The gallant "Russky" polkovnika with bandaged head and hand translated the first part, Madame Frank the second. The impression created by this brave woman, who had herself commanded a company in the trenches, was very great. There was no mistaking the effect of her words as these oil-stained workmen raised their paphas to the message from the English trade unionists which she delivered. It was in this vein that Colonel Ward and his party continued their campaign for the beleaguered workmen of Russia, many times fighting and averting*

*scorn from the Bolshevics. They continued to Novo Nikolsk, Barabinsk*
*and back to Omsk, where a lengthy report was given to Admiral Koltchak,*
*who expressed his hearty thanks and asked for a continuation of their*
*journey to the Urals, which began on April 5th. They had an escort of*
*Sergt. Major Gordon, in charge of twenty-two N.C.O.s and men.*

On 27th March Omsk detachment entrained for Vladivostok,
leaving the escort with the Colonel in view of proceeding to
Perm etc. We left Omsk on Sunday April 6th. Monday we
inspected iron mines at Toyon (Tumen). Continued our journey
to Ekaterinburg, where we arrived on Wednesday 9th April. We
had the privilege of visiting the town and saw the house where
the late Tsar of Russia was supposed to have been murdered.
Trains travel through the streets and a splendid market is to be
seen there. Cigs 2/6 a packet – 3 roubles. Departed on Friday
and arrived at Teghill (Taighill) on Saturday. Departed on
Monday arrived Queshwer (Kushva) Tuesday and Isver vit chev,
Wednesday. Thursday found us at Iswell, departed next day and
en route came across a mission from Archangel which appeared
to have had a rough time. The tale told is very pitiful, for men,
women and children have been cruelly murdered by the
Bolshevics, whole villages being wiped out. We took the party
back to Perm. The party consisted of a Serg't of the Durhams
and a few Russkys back to Perm, arriving there on Saturday
April 19th. Here the station and carriages were decorated with
evergreens ready for the Easter holiday, fireworks plentiful.
Typhus fever was raging, with serious results.

The river at Perm thawed and icebergs, houses and wood
galore and loose boats came floating down the river. Unable to
leave at appointed time owing to railway bridges washed away.
Arrived been at Ekaterinburg 28th April, when we came in

contact with General Knox and staff: Admiral Koltchak arrived Wednesday May 1st. Returned back Omsk Saturday May 3rd.

Monday 12th, sing-song at Y.M.C.A. (American), Wednesday 10th day out to Cossacks display (very good). Most of the escort were worse for drink. Pte. Smith and Sergt. put under arrest, the former wanting to fight the R.S.M. After the fun that followed, some returned by motors, others by horseback.

*Nevanisk is situated just over the European boundary of the Urals. Before the Bolshevic came it was a great iron centre, one firm alone employing three thousand workmen. When we arrived there the various works were practically derelict and its vast collection of machinery idle. The streets were deserted, and it was estimated that half its inhabitants had been destroyed. It was, and now it is not. The few remaining inhabitants were valiantly pulling themselves together. We talked to them and encouraged them to continue their struggle against the blight that had defiled their homes and country. Their hopes seemed to revive from our assurance of English working-class sympathy.*

*Typhus was raging in almost every house. Doctors had largely disappeared owing to the hatred of everybody with a bourgeois education.*

*We arrived next at Taighill, where the same effects had been produced, though on a smaller scale. The meeting at Taighill was a repetition of the others and we passed on to Kushva. This district is remarkable for the extensive deposits of iron and sulphur which seem inexhaustible. One huge hill has a store of about 8,000,000,000,000 tons, almost untapped.*

*We set off for Perm, with a stop on our way at the Vackneah Turansky Works. These works employed from four to five thousand men, doing everything from smelting to the making of engines, carriages. shells, guns etc., and were the best-equipped workshops we saw in the Urals.*

*The old regime did everything - nearly all this great mineral district was developed under the personal care of the Tsars. The Bolsheviks have destroyed the state control of these establishments, and already the bourgeoisie are casting hungry eyes upon this great industry and the Omsk ministers are rubbing hands over the loot they hope to collect during this transfer. How vain the hopes of those who looked to the revolution to develop public control of all natural resources.*

*At Turansky we picked up Sergeant Coleman, of the Durham Light Infantry, the only Englishman who weathered the journey from Archangel, with a party of Russians who had started from the north to try and get into direct touch with the Red Army. They had made a circuitous route and avoided the districts held by the Bolshevic forces, and therefore had nothing of interest to report to us. The whole party, under a Russian officer in English uniform, were attached to my train and taken to Perm.*

*While examining the damage done during the street fighting at Perm, we encountered a mob of the Red Guard who had marched over their own lines at Glashoff and surrendered to General Gaida. They were drawn up four deep in the market place for a roll call. I studied their faces and general appearance, and came to the conclusion that if the progress of the world depended upon such as these the world was in a very bad way. They were Kirghis, Mongols, Tartars and Chinese, mixed with a fair sprinkling of European Russian peasants, workmen and others mostly of the lowest types, but just enough of the "old soldier" element to make them formidable. A strange idea struck me that I would like to speak to these men. The proposition, made almost in jest, was taken seriously by my liaison officer, Colonel Frank, who interviewed the commandant of the station, Colonel Nikolioff, upon the subject. He at first took up a hostile attitude, but when he gathered the substance of my proposed address he consented, and arranged the meeting at the camp for 6 pm. the following evening, April 22. Of all the meetings it has been my privilege to hold, this was the most unique. The Bolshevic soldiers stood to attention and listened to me with great interest. One or two were sailors and some could understand a little English, as could be seen by the way they conveyed in whispers the points of the speech to their neighbours. Madame Frank translated, and in beautiful Russian drove home each point. Hers was a magnificent performance.*

*As she repeated my word-picture of their untilled fields, destroyed homes, outraged women and murdered children, not the ravages of an Allied enemy but the work of their own hands, Russian against Russian, tears trickled down their war-scarred faces. Clearly these men felt they had been deceived, and would willingly endeavour to rectify the injuries of the past.*

*Some volunteered their services at once to help their Mother Country to recover from the ravages they had made and administer justice upon those who had led them into madness, but Colonel Nikolioff asked them to remember that their crimes had been very great, and nothing but time could heal the wounds and soften the bitterness their conduct had created. Some asked that it should be remembered that they were not Bolshevic in principle, but had been forced to become soldiers in the Red Army, from which they could not desert until their villages had been captured by the Koltchak army, as their whole families, held as hostages for their good conduct, would have been massacred. This they asserted had been done in numberless cases where the families were in Bolshevic hands.*

*On April 24 the ice on the Khama started to move about 5 am. It was a very imposing sight. It moved first as one solid block, carrying boats, stacks of timber, sledge roads – everything - with it. The point near the bridge held for some time, until the weight behind forced some part down and crushed its way through in one irresistible push; the other part rose in its resistance and rolled like an avalanche. over and over, smashing itself into huge blocks which were forced into a rampart fifty feet high, when the enormous weight broke the ice platform on which it was piled, and the whole moved majestically off towards the Volga. Then one experienced the peculiar illusion of gliding along the river; it was necessary to plant one's feet far apart to prevent a fall.*

*At Perm the breaking of the ice revealed sufficient evidence of the callous behaviour of the Bolshevic administrators. Below a steep bank a few yards from the Terrorist headquarters a small shed was erected on the ice. It was called a wash-house, and during the day washing was done there. At night the place was deserted, but as a square hole was cut through the ice, it was an ideal place for the disposal of bodies, dead or alive. The people knew that after an inspection of the better class homes by officers of the Soviet, if there was evidence of valuable loot, the whole family would quietly disappear. If a workman protested against this violence he disappeared too, in the same secret fashion.*

*The ice in the shelter of the bank began to thaw, and while it did hundreds of bodies were taken from the river by the friends and relatives of the victims. We held a big meeting in the great railway works which created quite a sensation. We returned to Ekaterinburg on April 29 and were surprised to find that General Knox and the Headquarters staff had removed from Omsk and taken up position there. The Hampshires were about to move up; barrack and other accommodation had already been secured. The first echelon arrived the following morning. An Anglo-Russian brigade of infantry was in course of formation and seemed likely to prove a great success. It offered employment for the numerous officers and N.C.O.s who had arrived and for whom no proper place for work had so far been provided. It was truly a stroke of genius for* our *War Office* to flood us with officers and men as instructors for the new Russian Army, scarcely one of whom could speak a word of Russian! I feel sure the Russians and ourselves will get on well together, we are so much alike.

We returned to Omsk on May 3 to find that the snow and ice had given place to a storm of dust which crept through every crevice of one's habitation and flavoured everything with dirt and grit. The service of a British soldier on these special trips is not exactly a sinecure. The people at home who pay can be sure their money is well earned before Tommy gets it. The south wind sweeps up from Mongolia and Turkestan, and while it brings warmth to our frozen bones its blessing becomes a bit mixed with other things before we get them.

General Evan Pootenseiff arranged a parade of the 2nd Siberian Cossack Regiment outside Omsk on May 14 to say "Goodbye" to the "Anglisky Polkovnika", his officers and soldiers. Needless to say we were all there, and it was an occasion that will be remembered by all who had the honour to be present. The parade was under the immediate command of the Assistant Ataman, Colonel Bezovsky, and the wonderful display of horsemanship was loudly applauded by the English Tommies, who were most interested spectators.

The parade over, the officers adjourned to an extremely artistic Kirghis tent pitched on a treeless plain, where lunch was served; but the viands were left untouched until the toast of "His Britannic Majesty" had been drunk in good Tsaristic vodka. Then it became a real military fraternisation. Officers inside, soldiers out. No civilian was allowed to approach within three versts, except the old Kirghis chief, who dressed in his picturesque native dress had travelled over fifty versts to attend the function of making an English Ataman. The band of the Cossack regiment tried valiantly to enliven the proceedings with music, but the English marching choruses soon silenced all opposition.

*Then the Cossacks placed their commander upon two swords and tossed him while singing the song of Stenkarzin, the robber chief, and at the end drew their swords and demanded toll, which took the form of five bottles extra! I was then admitted to the fraternity and presented with the Ataman's badge, and after due ceremony with a Cossack's sword, by the regiment, admitted to their circle. I went through the sword tossing, and gained freedom for 100 roubles; and here my narrative of making of a Cossack had better end.*

*Thus having finished my work at Omsk, I asked that arrangements might be made as quickly as possible to transport my escort and myself to Vladivostok. The arrangements were completed by May 21, when I announced myself ready to begin the first stage of our journey homeward. The Supreme Governor surprised me by a visit to my carriage to say "Goodbye". He said my voice, my presence and influence had aroused the better elements to throw off the feeling of despair which had so universally settled upon them. I considered his visit and words the act of a gentleman, and as such I appreciated it.*

*I could but recall the last time he visited me, in the doubtful days of November, when I suddenly found myself in the presence of who had assumed the role of Dictator. Once having given my promise to help, he never found that help withheld at critical moments later. The British forces were few, but they were disciplined and knew their own mind, and this was what every other party, both Russian and Allied, lacked. Every Allied force had its "Politicals" at hand, and therefore were powerless for any purpose. The Fates had sent ours to Vladivostok, 5,000 versts east, at the very moment when their presence and general political policy would have paralysed correct military action.*

*Our journey east was broken at Krasnoyarsk, and passing Irkutsk, we again struck the Baikal - looking more glorious than before. In the morning sunshine the snow-covered mountains in the east pierced the heavens with the radiance of eternal day. As we travelled round under the shadow of these giants, the temperature fell many degrees below zero, and the cold from the water penetrated the carriages, necessitating fires and warm furs, in spite of the June sunshine.*

*About thirty versts west of Manchulli our train was stopped by a red flag, and a railway workman informed us of a raid upon a homestead by the side of the railway, the robbers having decamped two hours before our arrival. The father had two bullets through his chest and one through the right side of his neck, and had crawled a distance of over a verst to give information. He was taken up on our train, and we went forward to the scene of the tragedy. In the small wooden house, covered with loose feathers, lay the dead body of the mother with her unborn baby. Nearby lay a girl of about ten with her head terribly wounded. In an outhouse was the body of their Chinese boy. My hospital orderly rendered what aid was possible to the girl, who was carried by Madame Frank to my carriage for conveyance to the hospital at Manchulli. A civilian doctor declared both cases hopeless. It was entirely through the tenacity of the injured man that the scoundrels with the Bolshevic commanders in the area were identified.*

*It was June when we passed over the Hingham range, a series of sand mountains. Snow was falling in clouds and banked itself against the rails and telegraphs in a surprising manner, considering the time of the year. The summer of this wild region lasts about two months - July and August - during which time the sand becomes hot and travelling is not comforting.*

*From the Magazine*
*On Lake Baikal.*
*By George Butterworth, "L. Cpl. unpaid."*

The majority of us boys have seen this beautiful lake in two aspects and who of us can forget the first glimpse of that shimmering expanse of water, cold even in summer and for two fathoms deep, in winter, ice covering its immense surface .

The water of Baikal is wonderfully clear and cold at all times; surrounded by mountains and forests, the views obtained from the railway are unsurpassed.

Baikal is quite a baby. Oh no! Baikal was not there at one time, in its place, an area of about the same as England, were thriving villages, the peasantry of which sent vast supplies East and West. These villages were greatly noted in their day, for the peasantry were in the belief that the surrounding mountains were growing in height; their rumours spread over the country, until strangers from distant parts visited and explored most of the villages.

Among the incoming rush of sightseers was an engineer who having plenty of time at his disposals, stayed at Irkutsk, fitted up a caravan, and with a few followers started out to investigate. After four months' absence he returned to Irkutsk and astonished the authorities with the fact that the mountains were certainly gaining height, as the earth was gradually giving way in the valleys. This man produced measurements he had taken and proved that the ground was falling to the extent of half an inch every week. Again this man started an expedition of investigation, and after several trials, and narrowly escaping death, he discovered a mighty river, underground. Awed by the discovery of the river, hidden from the ignorant peasantry, and fearing a cataclysm, the brave engineer spread the news near and far, and was the means of saving thousands of lives. His warnings were at first ignored, but gradually the people awoke to the fact that it was true, and that the ground was actually sinking. A great exodus of people began, who established themselves on the surrounding uplands. A black day it was when the first village disappeared. Frantic with fear, the peasantry decamped without goods or chattels – some even now ignored the grave warnings and perished, drowned in their own homes.

Forty fathoms below Baikal, the forests, the homes and the people remain. The forests are there to be sure. Oh no! You must not imagine rotting timber, rotting vegetation – the forests, the flowers are there still, white, white like stone, for there they remain, petrified by the waters of beautiful Baikal.

Can you imagine an earthquake in Siberia? No, of course not, but still earthquakes are fairly frequent in winter. Irkutsk appears to attract earthquakes. The writer whilst in Krasnoyarsk, had the fortune to come in contact with M. Yudin, the possessor of the famous Yudin Library (now in Washington for safety). In fact M. Yudin was a pupil of mine, and the following was related to me by him. Mr. Yudin's grandfather was a very wealthy man, and owned a very successful gold mine, some 500 versts from Irkutsk. After one season's operations, his outfit was packed and proceeding with 900 poods of virgin gold to Irkutsk. The journey was extremely difficult owing to the cold, but fairly good progress was made to the shores of Baikal. The crossing to Irkutsk ordinarily at that time of the year was easy, and so Mr Yudin's grandfather found it, until about half way across, one of those fairly frequent earthquakes visited the spot. Almost immediately a great chasm appeared in the ice, and the whole expedition, men, horses, sleighs and gold, disappeared, disappeared beneath beautiful Baikal.

*After crossing the summit the plains fell gradually away, enabling the trains to move with great rapidity, and in less than two days we struck Harbin, and donned our topees and tropical clothes. At Nikolsk our train was stopped, as the No. 4 Post train from Vladivostok had been wrecked by Bolshevics, a startling situation considering that eleven months previously the whole power of Bolshevism had been destroyed in these maritime provinces. The station commandant was an old friend; he came into my car to explain how the cross purposes of the American and Japanese forces were producing a state of uncertainty and disorder as bad, if not worse, than existed under the Bolshevics.*

*Shortly before our arrival a detachment of the Red Guard had entered the station and, in the presence of the American soldiers who were guarding the station, had placed all Russian railway officials under arrest and the staff were told to leave their posts, as the Bolshevic army, with the sanction of the American Guards, was about to take over the line. Imagine my utter astonishment at this message, containing, as it undoubtedly did, evidence of co-operation and understanding between the Bolshevic forces and one of our Allies. I at once determined to make myself acquainted as far as possible with the policy of the American commanders. I found that both officers and men were most anxious to render all help possible to maintain Admiral Koltchak's authority and crush disorder in the far east and as they put it, "justify their presence in Siberia". Many felt that they were only helping the Bolshevics to recover their lost hold upon the people by providing neutral territory for Bolshevic propaganda; I learnt from these American troops and their officers and officials, from General Graves downwards, had been in actual correspondence with Red Guard officers, and that more than one understanding had been arrived at between them; that for a time the ordinary American soldiers thought the understanding between the two forces was so general and friendly in character that no further hostile acts were to be contemplated between them. It was true that this wrecking of trains and attacks on the line guarded by American soldiers made things look serious, but they felt sure that the confidence existing between the American and Red Guard Headquarters was so well established that these acts of brigandage could only be due to some misunderstanding. The Kravesk affair appeared to be only a symptom of a much wider policy, and not the foolish act of a negligent subordinate officer.*

*In one of my numerous interviews with Admiral Koltchak at Omsk he had made some very serious statements regarding the American policy in the Far East, which he feared would result in reproducing the previous state of disorder. I assured him that the policy of the Allies was to resist disorder and support order, and that I could not believe America had come to Siberia to make his task more difficult, but to help him in every reasonable way. He agreed that such was the intention of the American people, but he feared the American command was being used for other purposes. His officers had informed him that out of sixty liaison officers and translators with American Headquarters, over fifty were Russian Jews; some had been exiled from Russia for political and other offences, and had returned as American citizens, capable of influencing American policy in a direction contrary to that desired by the American people. I assured him that this could not be, and that his people might themselves in this matter be under the influence of a near eastern neighbour not friendly to American interference in Eastern affairs, and that under this influence they might greatly magnify the danger. My words seemed to ease the Admiral's mind, but he regretfully replied that the reports were so voluminous and categorical in character that he thought that I, as a representative of the people of England, as well as an officer of His Majesty's Army, ought to be acquainted with the situation.*

*Following up my inquiries there fell into my hands a letter, dated May 25, from the American Officer (Captain __ ) commanding the American forces at Svagena, addressed to the officer commanding the Red Guard operating in that district. The American addressed the Red Guard commandant as a recognised officer of equal military standing. The American officer complained that after a recent fraternisation of the two forces which had taken place in accordance with previous arrangements near the "wood mill", on the departure of the Red troops he received reports that the Red Guard officer had ordered the destruction of certain machinery at the mill, and had also torn up two sections of the line at points east and west of the station at Svagena. The American captain enumerated other accusations against the Red Guard, such as threats to bayonet certain orderly disposed people who wouldn't join the Bolshevic army, and warned the Red commissar that these acts were contrary to the agreement entered into by the chiefs of the American and Red forces and if such acts were repeated he would take steps to punish those who committed such breaches of their joint understanding.*

*I think this letter from the American officer at Svagena is positive proof of some local or general understanding between the American authorities and the Red Army operating in the maritime provinces, and further, that this understanding had existed for many months; that it was this understanding which prevented the American forces joining in the combined Allied expedition to relieve the besieged Russian garrison in the Suchan district; that under this American-Bolshevic agreement the small scattered Red Guard bands who were dispersed by the Allies at the battle of Dukoveskie in August have collected together and formed definite military units. In other words, that the American policy, unconsciously or otherwise, has produced a state of unrest amongst the Allies, and unrest and anarchy amongst the population of the Transbaikal* and Ussurie Provinces, which may prove disastrous to the rapid establishment of order in Russia. They have created plans and disorder which, if it does actually create a serious situation for themselves, will do so will do so for those Allies who are trying to bring order out of chaos. The reduction of the whole country to order, to enable it to decide its own future form of government, is as much an American as a British object. That some sinister underground influence has deflected American policy from this straight and honest course is quite obvious.

The American command declared a neutral zone in the Suchan district. Armed operations by Russian, ie. Admiral Koltchak's or Red Guard forces, were prohibited in this zone. Lenin and Trotsky's officers jumped at this order and at once began to collect their scattered forces together. Within three weeks they raised their Bolshevic flags on their own headquarters, under the protection of the flag of the United States. From this neutral zone the Bolshevics organised their forces for attacking the Japanese on the Amur, for destroying British and other supply trains on the Ussurie Railway, and finally exchanged shots with the Russian sentries near Vladivostok itself, always bolting back to the American Zone when attacked by the forces of the Supreme Governor.

The other Allies and the Russians, having got the measure of this neutral zone business, naturally took steps to protect their men and property, and for a time the operations of this very energetic Lenin officer were confined to robbing and destroying a few isolated villages in the Maritime provinces; but the utter absurdity of American policy was at last brought home to the Americans themselves. The Red Guard commandant, chafing under the restrictions imposed upon him by the Russian and Japanese forces (in which the British also joined when Captain Edwards could get near with his good ship 'Kent'), decided to attack the unsuspecting Americans themselves. The Red Guard were *very clever in their operations. The American troops were guarding Vladivostok-Suchan Railway; the neutral zone was at the extreme end of the line. If the Red Guard had attacked the end near the zone their tactics would have been discovered at once. They therefore usually marched out from the American zone, made a detour through villages and forests and struck the railway as far distant as possible. Destroying a bit of line - perhaps if they had good luck – burning a bridge - they usually exchanged a few shots with the American troops, and if pressed, marched back to the zone under the protection of a section of the very forces they had been raiding. The American command naturally became more vigilant on the distant sections of the line, and this forced the Bolshevics to operate nearer and nearer the protected zone; but in the meantime they managed to kill several Russian soldiers, wound a few Americans, and destroy five different sections of the railway. Then they operated too near the zone where, to add insult to injury, they claimed that in accordance with American proclamation they could not be molested as military operations were prohibited within the zone! Someone suggested a more comprehensive and bonding agreement was necessary between the American and Red Guard forces to prevent regrettable occurrences in the future, and a conference was actually arranged, but was dropped when the Supreme Governor's representative declared to General Graves that his proposed conference with the 'enemies' of the Russian Government would be considered as a hostile act. The breaking off of these negotiations caused great annoyance to the Soviet Government, and they ordered their commissars in Ussurie to use the forces which had been organised under American protection to attack their protectors, which they at once proceeded to do. This doubtless altered the relationship of these two parties, though the chances are that the powerful influence which forced the American commanders into this ill-fated policy will be powerful enough to prevent an open American declaration against the Reds in the Far East.*

*It is well at this stage to estimate the effect this American muddle has had, and will continue to exert, upon the effort of the Allies to secure some sort of order in the Russian Empire, and upon the position of the Americans themselves and their future relations with the Russian people. The American troops were spread over the whole province from Vladivostok to Nevsniudinsk, a point east of the Sea of Baikal. They were almost entirely confined to the railway, but in this country the railway is the centre and heart of all things. American policy at Vladivostok applied to the whole of this area, which is really the Transbaikal provinces, or all Siberia east of Baikal. In the early days of September 1918, when I passed with my battalion towards Omsk, this immense area had been reduced to order by the efforts of the Allies, at the head of which I place the gallant Czechs. The American forces arrived too late to take part in the military operations but began to settle down to the work of administration with energy and ability. The French moved forward after myself, and the Italian unit followed later, leaving the American and Japanese, with such isolated Russian forces as had called themselves into being, in absolute possession of Transbaikal Siberia. There was not a single band of Red Guards one thousand strong in the whole territory. After nine months of Allied occupation the Reds organised, largely under American protection, two divisions (so called) of from 5,000 to 7,000 men, and numerous subsidiary units of a few hundred, who murdered and robbed in every direction, and destroyed every semblance of order which the Supreme Governor and the Allies had attempted to set up.*

*It was a major mistake of England and France to leave America and Japan cheek by jowl without a moderating influence. The rivalries of these two powers in this part of the world were well known and should have been provided for. It was too much to expect that they would forget their concession and trade rivalries in a disinterested effort to help Russia. The work has therefore to be done over again, or the Allies, finding the task too great, may retire and allow this huge province, probably the wealthiest part of the world, to recede back to the barbarism of the Bolshevic.*

*This then was the situation in the Far East in June 1919. As I was leaving Vladivostok I heard that the Red forces that had been organised in the American neutral zone had at last boldly attacked their protectors. The Red Army finally triumphed, and by 1920 all resistance to the Reds had ceased except in outlying areas of the Caucasus and in Eastern Siberia.*

Departed Omsk the 23rd May, arriving at Krasnoyarsk 25th, Tiskas 26th, Irkutsk 28th, Lake Baikal 29th, departed 30th. Arrived Chita 31st, departed June 1st, arrived Chiota 3rd June, departed 4th, arrived Harbin 5th June. First train held up by a man who had been robbed by a gang of armed men. Train proceeded to the spot, where the officials found two dead, a man injured and an infant of three years battered about with a hatchet. C/O Burgess dressed the man and child and conveyed them to Manchuria Hospital.

Left Harbin 8th June arriving at Nikoliosk 9th, where more trouble awaited us. Spasskoe and district captured by Bolshevics. Express train to Vladivostok derailed by Bolshevics. Transport train laden with horses derailed between Krasnoyarsk and Omsk, falling over embankment 60ft, all killed including English and Canadian horsemen. Under orders to proceed to front at Nikoliosk 10th inst.

This tragic last paragraph, for the troubled Russian people and the work which had been done in vain against the Bolshevics, marked the end of the Diary of Private Bridges. But his story continues through the words of others, within the Regimental Magazine which resumed publication during the last few months' stay in Vladivostok, of the remaining troops while they waited for the ships to take them home to 'Blighty'. Among his possessions was the July issue of the magazine of his regiment and he became a civilian once more in October. He may have been one of the last to leave Russia, true to the form of being one of the last to leave the Urals. Nonetheless, he was among the heroes fortunate enough to go home in good health, and doubtless mourning from time to time the losses of some of his mates in the army.

*From the Regimental Magazine*
THE INTERVAL
A SUMMARY

Many changes have taken place since the old tranquil days of Hong Kong and Singapore, and during the year which has almost passed since the 25th Middlesex Regiment arrived in Siberia, its members have travelled far and gathered much new knowledge and experience of a more or less exciting nature. It is to attempt to carry on for ourselves the tale of the doings of the Battalion where it was broken off when the last number of the "Mag" was published in Hong Kong in July 1918, and to record some of the Siberian experiences, that our little journal is being restarted.

After very Children-of Israel-like departures from their

respective stations, the two wings of the Battalion arrived at Vladivostok on August 2nd. 1918, on board the S.S. "Ping Suie." After a few days' hard work, the disembarkation and settlement in East Barracks was accomplished. On August 5th a strong detachment under the command of Col. Ward proceeded up the line towards the Ussurie River Front, to "show the flag" and to give the much-tried Czechs visible evidence that Britain and the Allies were coming to their aid. The expedition, however developed into a much more serious affair than flag waving, and during the latter weeks of the months we had our first actual active service experience.

The memories of the bivouacs, the trenches and the mosquitoes, and the battle of Kriefski, must not be permitted to die away. Nor yet our railway-truck life and sojournings at Svwagenoff and Spasskoe. These times are the stuff which mellow with age, and above the recollections of the mosquito-infected nights and dew-sodden wood come the memories of camp-fire and bivouacs, the half-lit faces round the glowing logs, and the songs sung when the day was done. Here too at this time, we were able to understand and appreciate the sterling qualities of our Allies, the Czechs, resolute and brave men all, and as generous as brave.

September 1918 was spent in Spasskoe or on detachment along the line to the Ussurie River, but at the end of the month the battalion gathered its scattered forces together and began its 4,000-mile journey to Omsk, then the seat of the new Siberian government. We were fortunate in having fine weather during the whole of the month-long journey, and were privileged to see the country in all its autumn glory. The sections of the line through Manchuria and round the south of Lake Baikal lay through especially beautiful districts. Short stops were made at most of the important towns en route, and in many cases marches were made through the main streets. We were thus able to see something of Harbin, Chita, Irkutz and Krasnoyarsk.

At Zema, a small railway centre between Irkutz and Krasnoyarsk, the old 25th took part in an exciting little episode. On our arrival at the station it was found that the local Bolshevic element was in an aggressive mood and threatening to interrupt railway communications. Measures had to be taken to counteract this, and after "standing to" round the station all night, strong parties were detailed in the morning to make a house to house search through the town for illicit arms. Quite a number of rifles and old arms of all descriptions were found, and after taking this precaution the journey was continued. Krasnoyarsk was reached on the 20th of October and here to the mutual regret of all, "C" Company was left on detachment. The remainder of the unit proceeded on the 22nd. and after a few uneventful days travelling arrived at Omsk on the 26th. of October, 1918.

Our arrival at Omsk was marked by a most cordial welcome by the government and the people of the town. After the public reception the whole of the unit was entertained to dinner in the fine Cadet School. During the dinner the Mayor of Omsk, in the name of his fellow citizens, expressed his good wishes to the battalion, and the remainder of the evening was spent musically or in fraternizing as far as the language limitations would admit with our hosts.

Of our life at Omsk and Krasnoyarsk, little need be noted here, and it will suffice to say that although as a rule the time passed very slowly and monotonously it was not altogether without an occasional spice of excitement. Several attempts were made by the local revolutionaries to overthrow the government and return to the Bolshevic regime. The first of these occurred soon after our arrival, and was by far the most serious. Thanks, however to the loyalty of the Cossacks and the new Siberian Army, and the help we were able to afford, the attempts on this and each succeeding occasion failed. Whilst at Omsk and Krasnoyarsk the battalion experienced the full rigours of a Siberian winter, the thermometer registering as low as 40 degrees frost, Raumur calculation. This being translated into figures Fahrenheit is somewhere about 90 degrees frost. We were also introduced to that somewhat terrifying phenomenon, a real blizzard.

Our mid-Siberian experience ended in March and April. The three companies stationed at Omsk entrained on the 29th of March and "C" Company at Krasnoyarsk on the 24th April, 1919, both with Vladivostok as their destination, but both, be it said, fully believing that they were beginning the journey home. The two parties safely reached their journeys' end on April 11 and May 9th respectively, only to find alas that an early return to England was out of the question.

Since our arrival in Vladivostok the great question, the cause of many rumours and more leg-pulling, has naturally been the date of departure for "Blighty". At present however we are compelled to admit that we can give no definite information on the subject and must unfortunately still leave the matter in the hands of Dame Rumour and the wits, adding only very fervently ,"Oh, Let it be soon."

*From the Regimental Magazine*
OBITUARY
THE LATE PRIVATE A. TONGE, "D" COMPANY., 25TH
BATT. MIDDLESEX REGT

It is with great regret that we have to record the death of Private A. Tonge, "D" Company, which took place at No. 11 Stationary Hospital, Vladivostok, on the 17th May, from Pneumonia. Pvt. Yonge was first taken ill previous to leaving Krasnoyarsk but as he survived the journey alright to Vladivostok, it was hoped that he would pull through. Unfortunately, he later became worse and eventually died, his funeral taking place, with military honours, at the cemetery at Vladivostok. Our deepest Sympathy is extended to all his friends and relatives.

SIDELIGHTS ON TRAVELLING IN SIBERIA
BY L. CPL. H. C. SLINGSBY

I am afraid that my literary abilities - if ever possessed - since my stay in this country have, in keeping with the weather, fallen below zero. As the resurrection of the "Mag" however, is taking place with the advent of summer, I may be able to gather my scattered wits together and blossom out again. If only I could make the primary effort, it is quite feasible that I might continue to write to some length and spring upon you my great work entitled "Siberia, as I Have Seen It", amounting to some volumes. In the meantime I think a short review appertaining to travelling in this country will suffice.

Ever since my arrival in Siberia I have been brought into close contact with all sorts and conditions of transportation. In the first place I did not make my original entry into Vladivostok with the procession of the troops, but by a motor lorry loaded with baggage, and I was the top "package". Fortunately I was able to keep my position en route, not being jerked off, as some other packages were occasionally. But I received an awful jolting, first over the cobbled stones of the main street and then down an apology of a road with ruts galore where owing to recent rains the lorry eventually sank with its weight, axle deep in the mud, and had to be unloaded of its contents before it could be extricated and the journey completed.

The next time I had to go through the town I took advantage of the tramway system. Joining the tram at the starting point, I was able to obtain a seat, but the tram had not proceeded far on its way before it rapidly began to fill, and before it had got half way into the town, although the interior was crowded to excess, I verily believe there were more people clinging on outside than were riding inside! I do not think I should have been able to have stuck the journey throughout had it not been for some ladies with an attractive perfume!

Upon another occasion I had to go into the town, on duty, with one of the springless carts that act as transport to this battalion, a mode of conveyance which I would recommend to any person desirous of a real joyride. It is most exhilarating and a good cure for a liver complaint or other internal disorder. The thing that I lacked, however, was a good cushion, which should always be taken, otherwise the journey is apt to become painful before the end is reached.

A ride in a droshky is not too bad, but one is always fearful of being precipitated into the street when rounding corners or bumping over roads which apparently have only been cut out and then left.

During the winter, however, to skim over the frozen roads in a sleigh is really delightful, providing one is well wrapped up.

Chinese coolies in Vladivostok have a special contraption attached to their backs by which means they are able to carry heavy packages from one place to another. I have heard say that a certain gentleman, upon one occasion, having had a more than pleasant evening out, not being able to obtain a droshky, accepted this mode of conveyance to take him back home!

Whilst certain of the troops were stationed at Spasskoe I had to make one or two special journeys between that place and Vladivostok. Arriving at the station rather late, I was only able to find accommodation in a crowded third class carriage. The occupants of same were an assortment of the working class and peasantry and once the train was on the move all entered into an argument which became very aggressive as the train proceeded further, culminating by two of the chief aggressors coming to the point of blows. This was all very exciting, of course, but it was difficult for me to grasp the situation, not then understanding much of the Russian tongue: the only thing about the language that I could grasp was that it was "o'chen pluker." I was therefore glad when night-time came, and the offenders, wearied by their excessive eloquence during the first six hours of the journey, fell asleep and the noise made by so much shouting changed to that of snores.

On the return journey I secured much better

accommodation, sharing a compartment with a Japanese lady and gentleman, whom I found both to be inveterate smokers and very liberal with their cigarettes, as they kept me well supplied during the whole trip.

Another journey which I made by troop train to Spasskoe was notable for one special incident. The trains are not addicted to speed on this particular line and when a man dropped his tunic out of the wagon he was travelling in, it was not a difficult feat to jump out after it, although it was not imagined he would do this. However, he did so, and finding his coat, commenced to run after the train with a view to catching it again. I will not say that he caught it as that would be stretching the point a bit too far, but he made a very gallant attempt, nearly meeting with success, and not abandoning the idea until he had covered a mile or so. He eventually finished the journey by the next train.

In the old days at home we used to sing of a journey by the South Eastern and Chatham Line where one could get out and pick flowers by the way, but on certain journeys which we have encountered out here it has been found possible, when the train has suddenly come to a standstill, to arrange and play a football match during the wait!

If one steps into a slightly overcrowded compartment of a train in England, one quietly meets with the marked disapproval of the other occupants. Having this in mind it has often occurred to me as to what these persons would have to say if they had to travel in the manner the people do out here. On an ordinary passenger train there are usually only one or two 1st, 2nd and 3rd class coaches, the remainder of the train being made up with "ty-ploosker." A "ty-ploosker" is merely a box truck, packed always to its full capacity with all sorts and conditions of individuals, together with their baggage and food for the journey, and in such a manner they travel hundreds of miles!

The majority of us in this battalion have had some of these long journeys and know how to go on pretty well. To wash and polish up is generally fairly easy- to have a shave is sometimes a difficult problem. The latter is usually managed best at a stop. If one is in need of a shave and has an idea that a station is not far away it is as well to commence to lather and lather until the train stops, and then apply the razor! I myself have shaved on one or two occasions whilst the train has been on the move, but this is not always a good policy, as I once found out when I tried it near Lake Baikal. I was managing fairly well and was part way through my "crape" when the train burst into a tunnel and plunged the wagon into darkness! To make matters worse this was only the first of forty tunnels, following quietly in succession and having no lights. My predicament is better imagined than described.

Concerning train journeys, an experience worth recording is when this battalion was going through last year to Western Siberia. We were travelling at night and most of us were soundly asleep when we were all awakened by a series of violent jerks, which went on for some time until the train finally stopped, and then upon investigation it was discovered that a portion of the train had been lost somewhere on the line! We were then pushed back to the last station and after a wait of some length, the missing carriages eventually were brought on to us by another train which had picked them up on its way.

Before concluding this article I must refer to the adventure that befell the Detachment from Krasnoyarsk whilst on its way back to Vladivostok recently. On a certain portion of the journey, the train was being hauled by two engines, when suddenly much shrieking of the whistles could be heard, which continued for some time until the train eventually came to a standstill. Upon enquiring what was the matter we learnt that the leading pair of wheels of the train-engine were off the line and that it had been travelling like this, at a good rate, for about a mile or more. The driver could not pull up sooner because the front engine was still pulling until the driver of same was aware that something was wrong. The permanent was cut very badly and it was altogether a lucky escape from more disastrous results. Our interpreter put it down to the "Bolshies" again, but I do not think it was their doing this time, although we had passed train wrecks occasionally, the result of their work.

Congratulations. We tender our heartiest congratulations to Col. John Ward, Major F. J. Browne, Captains A. H. Smith, E. G. Eastman and J. A. Boulton on receiving the Honours by which His Majesty the King has acknowledged good work they have done during the war. Our Colonel is admitted into the Companionship of the Order of the Bath and the other officers mentioned have had conferred upon them the Order of the British Empire.

*From the Regimental Magazine.*
The Unveiling of the Allied War Memorial

On Sunday, June 1st, at the Marine Cemetery, Vladivostok, the monument erected to the memory of the Allied soldiers who had died whilst on service in Siberia was unveiled. Officers were present representing America, Britain, Bohemia. France, Italy and Japan. Among the British officers present were - Major General J. A. Elmsly, C.B., C.M.G., D.S.O., C.E.F.(S.); Lieutenant-Colonel A. A. H. Powell, C.E.F.,(S.); Lieutenant-Colonel C. G. Wickham, B.M.M.: Major E. Powell, B.M.M., and Major F. Browne, O.B.E., 25th Battalion Middlesex Regiment.

A firing party and band were provided by the 25th Middlesex Regiment. The 31st Regiment, United States Infantry band, and a detachment of the Canadian Expeditionary Forces (Siberia) were also in attendance.

The Officiating Chaplains were: Major McCausland, M.C. and Capt. J. O. Oliver; the band of the Middlesex Regiment played the hymns and responses. The services opened with the hymn "For All The Saints," sung by all present, following which prayers were given by Major McCausland, M.C.

The memorial, which was draped with the Allied flags, was then unveiled by Major-General J. A. Elmsby, C.B., C.M.G., D.S.O. The hymn "Abide With Me" was afterwards sung; the "Volleys" fired, and the "Last Post" sounded, and a very fitting and impressive service was concluded by the English-American Bands playing the National Anthems of the various Allied Nations.

J. B. Schatzen, Sergt.


LETTERS.


They are born beneath a blessing;
They are sometimes splashed with tears;
The golden laughter sometimes thro' them rings,

They are throbbing with the hopes and sometimes with the fears,
That are far above the plane of common things.
They are like the light at evening,
When the mist has hung all day:
And surely some enchantment in them dwells.
For they satisfy our longings, be they either sad or gay.
And are holy like the sound of far off bells.
H. P. Moorby.


Condolences. We extend our sincerest sympathy to the relatives and friends of the following of our comrades who have died in Siberia: Sergt. S. J. Webb died at Spasskoe, Sept. 14, 1918. Pvt. F. C. Wade died at Vladivostok, Sept. 16, 1918. Pvt. C. Harding died at Omsk, Nov. 20, 1918. Pvt. G. W. Crossley died at Omsk, Dec. 17. 1918. Pvt. J. Fuller died at Omsk, Jan. 16, 1919. Pvt. A. J. Martin died at Manchuria, Jan 22, 1919. Pvt. E. J. Cruse died at Manchuria, Jan. 9, 1919. Pvt. H. Wells died at Vladivostok, Feb. 8 1919. Pvt. J. Bungay died at Vladivostok, Feb. 9, 1919. Pvt. A. Tonge died at Vladivostok, May 17, 1919. G. A. Hamlyn died at sea on the S.S. Madras on the way home.

The simple and dignified verses by our Chaplain, the Rev. B. C. Roberts, C.F., which we print on another page, very beautifully express the verity and generosity of the sacrifice they have made, and we hope the thought will be some little consolation to those who mourn their loss. The comrades we have lost during the war are members of that great silent army of Britain's dead on whose graves the sun will never set.

*From the Magazine*

## IN MEMORY OF THE BRITISH TROOPS WHO DIED ON SERVICE IN SIBERIA, 1918-1919.

The Spirit of England Speaks:
Do Honour, Sister, to these sons of mine,
Born of my womb, and wedded to my fate:
Who flocked with lavish zeal to dedicate
Their lives at duty's love-ennobled shrine.

Saved once from wreck, and on the battlefield
Scatheless, for heaven willed them to escape:
At last in no less honourable shape
On bed of mortal pain their vows they sealed.

Sister, accept their gift; 'twas made to me:
I mortgaged it for friendship's urgent debt:
Say that their blood outpoured shall blossom
Say that again thou'lt wrestle to be free!

The Spirit of Russia replies:
O Island Queen, own daughter of charity,
Proud in thy sons, to that same virtue true:
I need thy gifts, I need thy pardon too:
Forgive, I pray, my seeming perfidy.

I was not false at heart, but forced astray:

Oppressed by fools, by charlatans misled;
Now by the name of these thy cherished dead
I pledge my honour once again today.

Here will I guard them, folded to my breast,
Until their God and mine shall bid them rise:
Then shall their souls be precious in His eyes
And I new-born rejoice to see them blest.

Siberia, 1919. B. C. Roberts, CP.

## BOXING

On Saturday, June 14th the boxing men of HMS "Kent" and the 25th. Middlesex Regiment turned out in full force to give an exhibition boxing programme, for the benefit of Russian Cadets in training on Russian Island.

The day was ideal, the sun shining strongly, with just enough breeze blowing to make boxing a pleasure. The competitors went over to the island in fine style on the pinnace of HMS "Kent".

At 3.30 sharp the bouts commenced. The ring erected in the open was surrounded by a very keen and enthusiastic bunch of spectators. Gunner Farthing, R.H.A., and A. B. Lucas started the ball rolling and gave a clean, good humoured 3-round exhibition . This was followed by Private Bayliss and A. B. Neighbours, both very clever and scientific fighters. Others who fought were "Jumbo" Adams, L. C. Manton, Boy Roberts, Smn. Brown and Smn. Small.

All the contests went off in fine style and everyone agreed that for science, speed and clean fighting it would be hard to find their equals. Smn. Denyer, known to all as one of the best at the "noble art", made all the arrangements, and was responsible for the matching of the competitors. This was done with conspicuous success.

After the contests the boxers, seconds and spectators who came from Vladivostok to witness the affair, were entertained by the N.C.O.s and instructors of the Russian Training School. A scrumptious dinner was laid out on tables erected on the lawn; beer and cigarettes were plentiful and everyone thoroughly enjoyed themselves.

The pinnace left the island at 6:30 p.m. amidst the cheers of the Russian Cadets.

The object of these bouts was to give the Russians an idea of English fair play and to show them that when a fight is finished no malice is borne. Everything was just A.1 and although out here in Siberia it proves that the good old manly sport is still going strong and flourishing.

Gunner H.C. Farthing, Royal Horse Artillery

A very interesting evening was spent at the American Y.M.C.A. on Friday, 20th June, where six well-matched contests were witnessed by an assorted crowd of spectators, consisting chiefly of members of the Allied forces. The Middlesex and "Kent" supporters were in full force.

A Friendly Match and an Evening's entertainment between the W.O.s., C.P.O.s of H.M.S. "Kent" and the members of the Sergeants Mess. By C.Q.M.S. G. E. Tatham.

On Saturday afternoon, the 14th inst., a football match was played at East Barracks, between the W. Officers and Petty Officers of H.M.S. "Kent" and the Sergeants of the Battalion, proving a very interesting match. The result was a win for the Sergeants by three goals to two.

At the conclusion of the match an adjournment was made to the Sergeants Mess at West Barracks where the W.O.s and P.O.s of the "Kent" were entertained by the Sergeants to a supper, followed by a successful musical evening. Altogether it was a very enjoyable day and the arrangements made for same proved very satisfactory.

A parting match between a team from H.M.S. "Kent" and one from the 25th Battalion Middlesex Regt. was to have taken place on Saturday, 21st June. 1919, likewise a match of fancy dress character, was to have been played between the W.O.s and P.O.s of H.M.S. "Kent" and the sergeants of the 25th. Bn. Middlesex Regt. To the bitter disappointment of all, however, wet weather prevailed throughout the day and both matches had to be abandoned.

In the evening of the same day, the P.O.s and W.O.s of H.M.S. "Kent", having "borrowed" the Sergeants' Mess at West Barracks, entertained the members of the latter to a dinner. Some of those present wore their fancy costumes that they had intended wearing during the football match, thus causing much merriment.

The rest of the evening was devoted to a smoking concert and jollifications, whilst at different periods, the band of the 25th Battalion Middlesex Regt, under Sergeant Fawthrope, rendered some excellent music. The commander and other officers from the ship paid the mess a visit during the evening, as also did Major F. J. Browne, Capt. and Adjutant A Henderson Smith, and Capt. J. A. Boulton, of the Middlesex Regiment. Altogether a very enjoyable time was spent.

## FAREWELL.

We have unfortunately to include in this, our first number in Siberia, our Colonel's farewell message to the Battalion on his departure for England. We assure him the regret he expresses is as sincerely felt by all who have been with him for so long. We too, had hoped that our long journeying together would only have ended when the 25th. Middlesex Regiment ceased to be. Other duties have, however, willed otherwise, and Colonel Ward leaves Vladivostok on the 21st. of June, 1919, en route for the old Country.

We add to our congratulations for the safety and success which have been his through so many dangerous and difficult duties, our best wishes for his future and hope he will enjoy a speedy and favourable voyage home.

## COLONEL WARD'S FAREWELL MESSAGE.

I have always intended that our parting should take place only when I had carried you all safely back to dear old England. Now, however, best friends commissioned my wish, but I go home, I and the care however, I leave much to my regret many of my oldest and best friends amongst the Officers, Warrant Officers, Non-Officers and Men of the Battalion. This is not my wish but like a good soldier, I must obey orders. Though I go home, I shall not forget your many kindnesses to myself, and the care of your interests will always be my first call.

It is my special wish that the wonderful and unique work which the Battalion has been privileged to perform in this world-shaking epoch should continue to be the pride of all who serve under its banner. Make friends with this great race with whom, for the time being, you are called to live. Share their joys and sorrows as friends and comrades, in the trouble through which they are passing, so best you can give aid to them and serve your own country. It has been your great good fortune that you were placed where you were able by your discipline and order to exert an historic influence upon the surrounding anarchy. Continue this influence and all will yet be well. Goodbye, and by these words I shake you each by the hand. - John Ward.


### THE DEPARTURE OF H.M.S. "KENT."


On Monday morning 23rd. of June, 1919, H.M.S. "Kent" sailed out of Vladivostok Harbour en route for England. Her company carried with them our best wishes for a safe and speedy voyage home, and for the future all they could wish for themselves. Short as the time has been during which the men of the Middlesex Regt. and the "Kent" have been together, it has been long enough, we feel sure, to lay the foundations of friendship and memories which will last long after the majority of our war experiences have faded away.

The morning broke warm and fine and one could fancy that

Dame Weather herself had put on her best behaviour to bid the good ship au revoir. At eight o'clock prompt the Allied warships in the harbour dressed ship in honour of the occasion and the necessary preparations were commenced for the departure. Among those who came to wish their many friends goodbye were General Hovart and his staff, officers of the Middlesex Regt. of the British and various other Allied missions and services, and a host of civilian friends and acquaintances which the ship's company had made during stay in Vladivostok. Guards of honour from the Russian School of Cadets and from the blue-jackets of the "Albany" lined the quay. Whilst, as was fitting, a launch had been chartered for the Middlesex so that they could escort their comrades a little way on their journey home, for a final send-off at the harbour mouth.

At nine o'clock the stern cables were slipped and shortly after the anchor weighed. Then as the ship moved slowly from her moorings came the deep-throated cheers and counter cheers, came the last shouted messages and farewells, came, with bands playing, the old familiar songs "For they are jolly good fellows," "For Auld Lang Syne" and all the old rags whose words mean so little but whose singing means so much; and finally came our last message from the "Kent" - "Goodbye and good luck Middlesex, hope you will be following us soon". Grey and graceful, with a ripple of white foam about her bows, she towered, a beautiful thing indeed, as with "paying off" pennant streaming in the breeze she began her voyage for England, home and beauty.

Surely the old band of the Middlesex Regiment never before played such inspiring music as, when perched in the bows of the little tug, we slipped down Vladivostok harbour with the good ship "Kent" on the morning of Monday, 23rd of June, 1919. From the shore could be heard the cheers of the detachments at West Barracks and Eggerschelt, and the whole ship's company sent back their answering cheers. Our last view of the "Kent" boys was a brave sight indeed. They crowded on the decks from fo'castle to quarterdeck, they swarmed the rigging, manned every point of vantage from the lowest port to mast-head, waving, cheering, singing, shouting to the last.

The departure of the "Kent" was an episode few of those privileged to take part in will forget. It was in epitome all the spontaneous good fellowship and mutual appreciation which has marked the very close intercourse of our two great services in this out-of-the-way corner of the world. Maybe at such moments we catch a glimpse of the spirit which has borne our race through so much "wrack and scaith", touch with our fingertips the garment-hem of the True Romance, and feel dimly the ultimate verity of that "Lovely truth the careless angels know."

*More from the Mag.*

## THE WOUNDED BEAR

This is Russia; the country of Cossacks and caviar. How it has descended from the luxurious land of the Romanoffs and Roubles to the chaos of Revolution and Ruin!

Russia needs our help and we are here to help Russia. Perhaps the first conclusion deduced from a cursory survey of the situation is the necessity for pro-Russian propaganda. In Europe this requirement exists, and probably in America also. In

England the essence of Public Opinion is "Why should we bother about Russia?"

In the Great War Russia was one of our "Gallant Allies" and the Great War is not yet over. The holocaust of wholesale butchery seems to be at an end but there still remains an infinitude of careful economic reconstruction to prevent the whole social system of the world being precipitated into chaos.

It has been said that Russia deserted us at a critical time and does not deserve our assistance. The fact is, however, that Russia gave us inestimable help at the start of the war when we needed it most. As for the subsequent desertion, the most superficial study will show that the Russia of today is the result of the terrible set of circumstances and events that led up to and culminated in the revolution.

What do you mean by "Russia?" Is it the land and the people or is it the Government - or the lack of it? The country has an enormous area, an enormous population, enormous natural resources and enormous possibilities. The people have been unfortunate in that their despotic government was a devitalizing ulcer in the life of the nation.

When the European war opened, Russia was one of the first in the field - Russia the Colossus, the Steam Roller, the Great Bear. How we were thrilled to read that she could put five million men into the fight. We accepted her efforts at par, as a matter of course. We were so engrossed in our own war efforts that we neglected to analyze the work she had attempted and the tools she had available.

The Allies in France and Belgium had a battle-front of about five hundred miles with comparatively good transportation facilities for men and material. The Russian battle-line extended over a thousand miles and she had marshalled against her almost half of the most effective German Army.

She was hemmed in at the Black Sea, the Baltic and the White Seas. The open port of Vladivostok was about six thousand miles away. Think of that! Six thousand long, weary miles away. The Trans Siberian Railway was the only artery of transportation.

The soldiers were very badly equipped and battalions of them went into the fight with their bare hands - and battalions of them died, died that the other Allies might the more easily stem the tide of Germans on the Western Front. In the meantime the governmental parasite continued to gnaw at the vitals of the nation. Russia fought like a giant shackled hand and foot. The amazing thing is that she fought so well and continued the fight so long. She expanded a prodigious effort against enormous odds to help save the world from the slimy tentacles of the German octopus, and she continued to do so for many years.

Contrast these conditions with the comparatively ideal situation on the Western Front, where the governments were behind the army and the transportation systems on land and sea were working with the precision of machinery. The Revolution was inevitable. It was the French Revolution all over again. It was the inexorable swing of the pendulum from the tyranny of despotism and Czarism. It is like a great chemical reaction that gives off its heat, light, vapours, odours, by-products and finally subsides into a new formula. It is a monstrous human equation- however complex- and must work itself out to a logical conclusion. The gigantic system of matter and energy that was the Imperial Russian Empire is entitled to our best skill to guide i's inertia and momentum to a modern democracy.

The Russians are really very fine people. They are not the barbarians that some would imagine. They are of the Caucasian race and their northern environment makes them temperamentally similar to the English-speaking nations. they have their own little idiosyncrasies, it is true. They like a slice of lemon in their tea and a taste of vodka in their wood–alcohol! But they are really human and subject to the same hopes and aspirations, failures and disillusionments as the rest of the world. They feel poverty, cold and hunger as well as you or I.

If for no other reason than pure commercialism, we should assist them to create an orderly economic system. They have unlimited raw material that is required in our industries and they offer an extensive field for our manufactured articles. Also we have a lot of money invested in Russia that would be very nice to have some security behind.

But the most imperative reason of all is simply that we must live in the same world as Russia - the hand cannot work independently of the arm. In her present state she is a powder magazine on the front lawn of civilization – a wounded bear on the rampage. She must be trained to live at peace with herself and the rest of the world with whom she is inseparably co-ordinated.

Sometimes in our more precipitate judgement we express impatience that we should be kept here to "do guards that are unnecessary," while the miners and the shipbuilders at home are playing fast and loose with the work that should be ours.

It may be admitted that considerable hardship is thus imposed - especially on the gallant veterans, some of whom have been away from their families since 1914 and longer. However we must bear in mind that the world is just emerging from a stupendous task well done and it would be tragic to take any chances that might jeopardise the fruits of complete victory. We must be patient just a little while, for we are now on the home stretch, the interval that is bestrewn with the obstacles that must inevitably follow in the wake of any such prodigious social upheaval as the war has been.

We have a tendency to accentuate our own inconveniences and minimize the troubles of our friends. We see the situation through the lenses of the moment. The powers that be have infinite difficulties of which we are unaware, and are handling a very delicate situation with tact and skill.

C.Q.M.s. MacMillan (R.E.), Attch'd 25th Middlesex.

## A PERPLEXING PROBLEM
### For Puzzling People of Prophetic Pretensions

What, in my estimation, is a great question for Optimists and Pessimists, Prophetic personages and far-sighted people, I am now placing before you, for free opinions.

I refer to the man of the future. The war has made a break in the lives of a great many men, who have joined the Army for the duration of the conflict, and I sometimes wonder whether the change will affect the majority upon their return to civil life.

Let us review the situation. For example we will take the case of a young married man with an average berth. Before the war, when he was at home, upon hearing the alarm go off in the morning, he would casually turn out of bed and commence his toilet, whilst his wife would rush downstairs, get him a good breakfast, and eventually send him off to business with a loving kiss.

Then the crisis came, his country needed him, and he joined the Army. The Reveille takes the place of the alarm, and disturbs him from many a pleasant dream. He gets up. Having no wife now to make his bed and perform other domestic duties, he must necessarily do for himself. He gets no loving kiss upon turning out for parade. More likely an unlovely look if he is at all behind. At the call of "Cookhouse" by the Bugler, he hurries to the Mess Room, with knife, fork and spoon, and partakes of the rations due to him. And so I could go on enumerating the various incidents in the routine of a soldier's life, but as you all know them so well, to continue with same would undoubtedly be a waste of time.

The point is, will this same young man – or he may have grown old by the time he gets his "ticket" – stick to the ways of the Army upon his return to civil life?

If he has been used to camp life, with only the bare ground or tent boards to sleep on, will he, when he gets back home again, want to sell the bedsteads and sleep on the floor? Or if he has been used to the trenches perhaps he will make himself a "dug-out" in the garden and employ a big drummer to create a din outside, so that he will not forget too soon the life he has lately left behind him. A quiet life all at once might upset him! On the other hand, should he decide to retain the bedsteads, will his wife be surprised if he insists on making the bed himself, immediately he turns out of same in the morning? Will he also insist upon the early morning tea or "Gunfire" and grouse if his wife fails to let him have a couple of biscuits to partake with it? Another thing – will he want to go through a course of physical drill before breakfast?

Then at meals, will he want to do without a table cloth? Will he want the tea brought to the dining room in a bucket or a "dixie", instead of a tea-pot, and will he want to drink it out of a basin, instead of a cup? Will he always want buns upon the table and also insist upon the larder being well stocked with same, as a reminder of old times? Will he always carry his knife, fork and spoon about with him and, upon the completion of each meal, wipe them clean on the nearest available article? And just to amuse himself, will he take advantage of an opportunity to throw a morsel of the fragments that remain at his wife, for sport?

When he goes off to business will he insist upon using dubbin on his boots instead of blacking or polish? And if it looks like rain, will he want to carry his overcoat strapped to his back? But if the sun shines brightly and there is every appearance of it being hot, will he want to turn out in navy blue or tweed "shorts," with putties to match? Will he carry his walking stick or umbrella at the trail or slope, or will he have a sling attached so that same can be carried at ease?

When at business, at the end of the week, when he has reaped the reward of his labours, going back into his soldierly habit, will he insist upon saluting for same? Will he hasten home each night so as to be indoors by 9.30 pm, failing which his wife may give him a lecture or even "C.B." for a week? Should there be an occasion when he would like to stop out later, will his wife give him a special pass to do so?

Will his wife receive a shock if her husband, once a week, lays his entire outfit and belongings on the bed, in neat array, following up in civil life the usual practice of a weekly kit inspection as when in the Army?

I have now supplied you with a number of queries. You may know of more in connection with the matter. In any case, my comrades, just conjecture it up in your mind, and I have no doubt but what you will agree with me that there are some funny times in store for wives, mothers, aunts, landladies, servants, charwomen, etc., etc., when we are back again in a collar and a tie!

## PRIVATE BRIDGES' RETURN TO THE UK

During the remaining weeks while the men of the Middlesex Regt waited to sail homeward bound, there was anticipation, sadness and disappointment to encounter. Following the farewell to their revered and respected Colonel Ward, and the send-off two days later for their comrades of H.M.S. "Kent", the anti-climax at the end of their months of travel and terror along the Trans-Siberian Railroad was in evidence. After the memorials and parades, the bugles and bands united the Allies in a common bond. Comparative calm had been restored to the units. The waiting game was played within the football matches and boxing contests, setting ally against ally in friendly rivalry.

If the men were impatient, it was only natural. Private Bridges had long since established his own philosophical mode of life; he kept his mind busy and his body fit by practising in the football teams. Instead of fretting away his time in waiting to go home, he spent each day with measured enjoyment working through his routine duties, easing himself from one day to the next, and taking pride in the moment's task.

Before Alf joined the Army he had developed these qualities

as a marathon runner, becoming known for his endurance and enthusiasm, which had enabled him to finish in all the long-distance events that he entered. This enthusiasm had led him into scoring, umpiring, arranging and scribing for the teams and clubs wherever he played. As a soldier he wrote of the successes of the Company teams and the Battalion team with pride. He enjoyed the challenge and the triumphs; the strength of his limbs and the freedom of running and kicking was the liberation of the spirit he held in check in all other facets of his life. His moments of elation came amid the cheers of the crowd, for when they all yelled with joy he was able to yell in unison with the crowd while his excitement soared. The emotions he couldn't show in company were safely liberated within the crowd of spectators.

Among his papers was the very dog-eared photograph, creased and soiled, of Alf, sitting cross-legged on the ground, in the front row of the English football team, and with it his "Notice" for being selected to play in the championship match of Vladivostok.


NOTICE

Football match


A football match will be played for the Championship of Vladivostok, on the Race Course Ground on Wednesday 13th. instant, between 25th Middlesex Regt. and the Phenic. Kick off 6 pm. Lorries will be at West Barracks at 5 pm. Band will be played during intervals. Team selected to represent the Middlesex:

Pte. Edmunds.
L/Cpl. Manton. L/Cpl. Fitzgerald.
Pte. Bridges. L/Cpl. Ashton. Cpl. Jones.
Pte Hall. Pte. Pinnington. Pte. Bayliss. Sgt. Roberts. Pte. Small.

Even if, in the Army, there was time to spare, there was no room for words to spare. An order was an order, though one like this was an honour to get. To be chosen for the team carried its own accolades; the congratulations and admirations would come later when the team had given its all to play the game fair and square to victory; or in defeat to concede as a gentleman would. Only in war is it a fight to win, for in sports there is always a fighting chance. No foul plays.

All good things (and bad) must come to an end. Another beginning arrived and again they pulled up stakes. This new journey long awaited eventually was begun. Those war weary soldiers were at last going home, and probably all vowing they would never leave old England's shore again. One never did, I know; in later years I heard him say "I've seen it all - been all round the world – there's nothing else you could show me. This is my home, it's a palace to me and I never want to leave it again."

He was right, he had been all round the world; the final journey took him from Vladivostok across the great Pacific Ocean to Vancouver. After a day or two of rest and sight-seeing, they entrained for the long and picturesque journey over the Canadian Rockies. Presumably the train paused at Calgary as there is a card which reads:

Welcome Home!

Greetings from
Calgary Branch Canadian Red Cross Society
Assisted by
8th. Field Ambulance
Women's Volunteer Reserve Corps.

The miles of tall pines must have been reminiscent of the journey along the Baikal Sea in Russia, with the glacial formations and the snow-capped mountains serving a chilling reminder of Siberia in the winter time. But compared with the sites in Siberia, the bullets and the blizzards, what more could the soldiers see in vistas of forests while the memories of Africa, India, the Far East, hot sun, tropical rains and tempests, mosquitoes, diseases and deaths, were still fresh in their minds. What more could impress them?

The Prince of Wales was in Winnipeg. There was fanfare and a parade and inspection. Was that the occasion of July 19? Another memento of Pte. Bridges is a programme of relay racing events, high jump, long jump, hurdles, pole jump, and throwing the javelin and hammer. The contestants are listed under such headings as B.E., (Australia), (N.Z.), (Canada), (S.A.) and U.S.A. The front cover of the programme bears the picture of the Prince of Wales below the crossed flags of Great Britain and Canada - mere conjecture on my part, I stand open to correction. In any case the occasion was undoubtedly an important and happy omen for the men who had been estranged from their own Royal Family for so long, to feel the warmth and loyalty once again.

Little has been recorded with regard to the movements of the 25th Battalion Middlesex Regiment at the end of their tour. Your indulgence in my last assumption is all I ask, while perhaps some one of my readers might be able to furnish a more factual timetable for the sake of history. Nonetheless, the journey was continued by rail to Montreal, where a ship was waiting to take them across the North Atlantic ocean to Glasgow, Scotland, and then to barracks in England for demobilization. For Private Bridges this was formalised on October 20, 1919, and the official stamp is marked "Hounslow". He probably went home a little while before then and was mailed the Army Form W.5065, which gives information under headings:

| Soldiers Earnings: | £ | s. | d. |
|---|---|---|---|
| 28 days' furlough at 2/6 | 3 | 10 | – |
| 28 day's ration allowance | 2 | 18 | – |
| Stoppages and Payments: Advance at Dispersal Station | 2 | – | – |
| Paid by demobilization postal draft Date | | | |
| 19.10.19 | 1 | 10 | – |
| 26. 10 19 | 1 | – | – |
| 3 . 11. 19 | 1 | 18 | 4 |
| **Total** | **6** | **8** | **4** |

Surely this meagre sum will seem poor reward for devotion to duty. Undoubtedly by their true patriotism and in humble gratefulness at being the lucky chosen ones to come home unscathed, their scant fortunes may have seemed enough to carry on with until they got a job and started back in civilian street.

Uncle Alf was home after going round the world. He turned in his gear and returned to St. Albans. His brother Bert did not come home from the war; his name can be seen on a memorial stone set in the wall in Verulam Road. As is the way with time, wounds were healed, mourning was done, and the war was put to the back of the minds of the people; and Alf hung on to the memories by hanging three pictures on his bedroom walls which remained there for the rest of his life, some sixty years more.

One picture was long and large; it was the "Roll Call of the 25th Battalion, Middlesex Regiment, after the sinking of the "Tyndareus"." The second, very wide and shallow, of the men in "D" company, five rows deep with forty-two men in a row, lined up beside and behind their divisional officers. The third picture is of the Commonwealth Flags embroidered under the crown and above the picture of Private Alfred Arthur Bridges; the message it bears is "Victory to the Allies".

Work was hard to find, and industrial strikes caused a further setback to the nation. Hunger and shortages plagued society for several years. Even so, in October Alf went before the Employment Board, to be callously told by one of its members, "Your Father is my gardener, he must keep you out of the wages he gets from me". So much for "When Tommie comes marching home". Days must have been long and depressing while Alf tried to find work; in this he had little success. He kept up his running and sports though, and his successes in these became awards and trophies which he stacked in a cupboard and polished at times when the silver looked dull. His energies spent in competitive sports compensated for the lack of the companionship of a woman.

He aged slowly while he kept up his training, though to my husband, who spent a good deal of his boyhood in Alfie's home, he was always grown-up and the same; quietly busy, doing his books, coming and going to either the billiard hall that he ran, or to the park or the pitch for football and cricket matches. There was little he did around the home as the bachelor son. Gran always took care of that till she died. Only once can my husband recall a time he saw Alf with a paintbrush in hand. That was to write John's name on his tuck box before he could be sent off to school. He was serious and glum then and trying to show that he cared about the terrible wrench John was feeling while he was such a little boy. Alf was to say in his later years as we painted his house up for him, "Can't abide the smell of paint, makes me sick you know. Gits caught in my throat and makes me cough all night."

He would soon disappear to the club after tea, to keep out of the way while the cleaning-up was done, at the times when the decorating was underway. There he would stay until way past midnight doing his bit among friends and cronies. For years he was the secretary-treasurer of the Camp Liberal Club, and eventually entertainment manager. To get there he walked, right up to his older years, turning down offers of a lift almost until the very end.

Back in 1936 he borrowed some money to buy three billiard tables and opened a billiard hall. He helped his old parents but made little money; he was always off to more rewarding scenes, to play in a match or to run. It was then that his sleeping habits were probably firmly established, long evenings were spent minding the boys, teaching them some of his skill with the cue, selling them buns and a cuppa and finally closing the till and locking the door after hours.

It was home to bed late, and sleeping till ten in the morning. A shave at the sink, Brylcreem on his hair, breakfast, and off to the Hall. Gran sent up his dinner, in a bowl and a bag, first in the care of young brother Don, and next in the hands of John, when he was home from school.

His business was busy during the war, the Second World War, that is. By now he had moved over Burtons the Tailors, a convenient spot near the middle of town where the Tommies and Yanks and the local cadets could meet for a sociable evening. No woman was seen in this man's domain, while the police had respect for discretion. There were always the limits to which Alf would allow, and after that, "Out you go boy".

After the war he raised three hundred pounds and purchased the house from the landlady to safely ensconce his old dad and mother for always. Dad passed away first and old Mum or Gran followed a year or two later. His house was truly his castle. Solid, old-fashioned, dark and damp in winter, steps down to the basement and two flights of stairs to the bedrooms. The loo was outside the back door. Before fuel became so expensive and hard to get during the war, the house may have been comfortable once, with all the fireplaces, one in each room, and the range in the scullery plus one in the kitchen as well. Across the corner to the left of the window was the huge bricked-in copper. The plumbing was one big brass tap hanging over the big square sink.

Nine months in a railway car, with a bucket for washing, no

lights, boarded bunk beds, food from a kit and a dixie made no. 105 look like a palace. He hadn't ever known the luxury of a bathroom, locked door, warm towels, a thick rug and somewhere to leave the soap. Always he'd managed to keep himself clean "without them new-fangled things"; a square spotty mirror propped up on the sill and the Ascot to warm up the water with a whoosh suited him down to the ground.

Every summer we came home from America, and stayed there to be with John's mother, who kept house for him, and sometimes at Christmas time too. He used to say "My home is your home, come whenever you want", and later he talked of modernising with an extension and bath for his "American visitors", but that never came off. Oh how he wanted to please, so mostly he kept out of the way, and turned up for meals on time. A creature of habit he was, tea and biscuits in bed, long years after he'd retired from business. Pop to the shop for the paper, and back for dinner at one. Nearly all afternoon he was in the front room where the trophies stood and watched all the sports on the "telly". Sometimes he wanted his tea on a tray, boiled egg, bread and butter and biscuits, then his fancy would change and he'd join us downstairs in fish paste and cress, and jam sandwiches, finishing up with a bun.

Alf and I would joke together, and on rare occasions he would wink and call me "my dear". Once I said how I missed the taste of the English blackberries, while we were sitting at dinner. He was more than eighty years old by this time, with knees swollen and sore with rheumatism. In the winter he turned his wheelback chair around from the head of the table, and sat as close to the fire as he could, until he could smell the heat of his old suit, and then he would shift back again, stand up and shuffle to his chair in the corner and doze off for a few minutes.

But now it was summer, the sun quite hot, and my reminiscing on picking blackberries as a child must have jogged his reverie too. Later that afternoon he was not home for tea, and we stood at the gate anxiously peering down the road, looking for him to turn the corner. He'd been gone a few hours, and as he finally approached his brow was wet and his basket was full, and he was smiling triumphantly.

"Have to know where to find them these days" he said, and told us whereabouts that was. A good ten miles there and back: With the standing and reaching, bending and stretching, the bees that buzzed around him and the brambles that caught at his sleeves and his wrists, he was tired out, but I'll never forget the look on his face. "For you, my dear" was all he said. Then he turned his back on me shyly.

Sometimes we'd tease him and offer rice pudding for sweet. "I don't want any of that!" he'd say in disgust, "Had more'n my fill in the Army, I'll never eat it again. Sausages too, horrible things made from all what's left over. We lived on rice in Singapore and bully beef and sausages in Siberia, can't bear to look at them any more." Oh Alfie, if only I'd asked you to tell us more, how enriched our lives would have been. You had to die before I read of the places you had seen.

The winter of '79 had been bitterly cold and the old folks were feeling the pinch. Uncle Alf came down with bronchitis, and in the spring he was really no better.

We received a phone call from my husband's sister. She had struggled for months to perk him up, but he seemed to be failing all the time. It was Easter week when I took a flight home to see if I could help in any way. When I arrived he was wrapped in a blanket propped up in a chair by the fire. What a change, no more rosy cheeks from the wind and the sun, and no interest in anything at all. The next day, as I made him comfortable and made his bed, he beckoned me to come closer, and looking straight at me he said, "I've had enough, I'm packing it all in". I knew what he meant, but had to be certain I'd heard right, so I said gently, "Do you mean you want to die, Uncle?" Then he put out his hand so I held it and said, "John will be here soon. he is hoping you will get better, play cribbage with him again."

"No" he said, "not any more, I'm old and tired and there's no more I want to do."

After that he gradually became weaker. He asked for a shave, so I gave him one and he took my hand to say thank you; then he realised we were holding hands and he slipped his fingers away from mine in embarrassment. He refused foods more and more and his voice became less and less audible. The doctor couldn't say how long he had left, so we called the relatives to see if they wanted to say goodbye. After they had left and one week to the day after I had arrived, John's sister and I sat by his bed touching him, checking his shallow breathing. Finally he closed his eyes as if to sleep, and he never woke up again. He died the way he had lived, quietly, with no fuss, and very little emotion, an old soldier faded away.

Because he had made no will, the house and contents had to be split up one way and another, and at this task we found his diary. As we read it we were drawn closer to Old Uncle Alf than ever we were while he lived. His souvenirs from the Army were no longer musty old pictures upon the wall, they were symbols of his youth when the world was young and there was hope for better things to come; not the fear of a world destroyed.

When his obituary was put in the paper (Alf wouldn't read it – "Mug's game" he'd say) I was willing to bet that hundreds of people would read it and say, "I see old Alf Bridges has gone!" They would have conjured up memories from years ago in lots of different ways. Not many people came to his funeral; one or two old pals and his latest friends, and the relatives who'd always known him. Any more and he would have been embarrassed to be the cause of so much fuss.

Alf will be remembered by few as a soldier, for most of the men he sloped arms with he has joined on more celestial manoeuvres. Some will recall his billiard hall, but more will remember the sports club member. From even before the Kaiser's war he ran in long-distance races. "In 1920" an old friend said, (in a letter from W. C. Brooks) "he was one of the senior members. The Elstree Club specialised in long distance road races, mostly held during the winter months. They also held a sports day on August Bank Holidays, and Alf was always there, usually with new recruits from St. Albans."

The St Albans club was started in about 1928 and Alf was a founder member. A starter and steward, a timer and judge, respected, admired and dependable.

Affable Alf – I can see him now, strutting down the street busily on his way there and back, in rain and shine. Passing the time of day with a cheery grin to neighbours and faces familiar. Well-known Alf, known well enough to be almost a permanent fixture, somehow part of the scene. Then time makes a change and little by little something goes, and he became part of what's gone.

Only memories now, of one of a group of folks from a gentler generation. Of people who preached and practised restraint and good manners and who slowly accepted change. Yet they saw many changes, new discoveries, rapid developments; one thing after another like domino chips, not falling in each other's wake, but marching in lines and veering off in many different directions. The locomotive steam engine was moving imaginations and materials faster, connecting the cities efficiently. Coal gas lighted the streets at night and glowed in the homes. Gas mantels started with a match and a poof, hissing and sputtering; turned off with a pop before bed. Cooking was easier too on a stove, ranges were hidden by boarding the hob into the chimney recess.

Then motor cars, gramophones and the crackling crystal set. At least two wars, boy scouts and semaphore. Silent movies, the telephone, "talkies" and the radio. Photography, electric light and vaccination. Jubilee and abdication, Coronation, celebration. The Great Depression, Crystal Palace, buzz bombs and the Blitz. Armistice Day, D-Day, V. E. Day. Splitting the atom, The Bomb and V. J. Day.

Medical breakthroughs and open-heart surgery, organ transplants and a man on the moon. Stereos, satellites and silicone chips. A world expanded now with a population explosion and travel by jet, a world controlled by computers and codes and plastic credit cards.

All of those things and more intruded upon their simpler times while often I heard it said, "There is nothing new under the sun". In war they fought for these things and in peace they sometimes fought against them, yet took them in their stride as a myriad of marvels in a world progressing to brighter and better things. The irony now and the fear of many is that we've come too far and too fast. We could ruin the lot in one hasty push of a button.

In the meantime I remember Alf and Uncle, Mother and Dad, Gran and Granddad, Auntie and all who went before to pave the way for the luxuries we have today and take for granted.

To complete the book, I must say I did not intend to talk of battles and politics, but in my research there were many opportunities for telling in detail the heroic deeds and triumphs of the soldiers. I read the book so ably written by Colonel John Ward and quoted above, "With the Die-Hards in Siberia", and was stirred by his explanations of the politics and the descriptions of the battles they fought.

In an effort to bring credibility to the words of Alf, a humble Private, it was necessary to use passages from his Commanding Officer's book and to interpret at times his story. This liberty was taken with the sincere intention of heralding the courage of the men of the 25th Battalion, Middlesex Regiment, "B-Oners" who stood like the best.

Colonel Ward led his men into hand to hand combat. He gave inspiration to his men and held empathy for their needs. Beyond that his honesty and fair dealings in a field of corruption set the examples of pride and decency among his officers and men.

The reader may have spotted some minor deviations where the dates of events in Siberia did not quite coincide. But it is well to note that while Colonel Ward was writing a daily log for posterity, it was part of his job to keep accurate accounts. In the case of Private Bridges, his story, spasmodically written, was penned after his other duties were completed. He recalled specific events whenever he had the time; or maybe at night if excitement invaded his rest or haunted him until he shared it with his diary. The trauma that gripped some of his days of terror and war was eased leaving him able to sleep.

At the time when Colonel Ward was made an Ataman, his story sings with a subtle humour and his sophistication left unsaid the outcome of his rejoicing with the Cossacks, but the private could see the funny side of the drunken condition of the private who wanted to fight the Regimental Sergeant Major!

Another interesting episode got me to thinking of two reports given by one man upon the same subject to two different audiences. Sergeant Coleman told the Colonel what he knew of where the enemy lay. The circuitous route by which he had travelled left him with "nothing to report." When he joined the men later the tale he then told was of the murderous Bolshevics and men, women and children cruelly treated and dead.

Private Bridges made another entry into his diary, and one or two more, while on the way back to Vladivostok, when he probably thought the journey was almost over. He closed the book then for more than three-quarters of a century. It is open at last with the story told and his journey truly completed.

### The End -

ND - #0441 - 270225 - C6 - 203/127/17 - PB - 9781861512567 - Matt Lamination